Morfudd Richards opened her London restaurant, Lola's, in 1996 after working at some of London's finest restaurants, including Le Caprice and The Ivy, and managing Marco Pierre White's restaurant, Harvey's, when it first opened in 1987. Morfudd and her business partner ran Lola's for ten years, during which time they established it as a neighbourhood favourite and in 1997 received the Time Out 'Best New Restaurant' award, as well as numerous other accolades.

In 2004, Morfudd was browsing eBay when her eye was caught by a 1970s ice-cream van. She bought the van, refurbished it, sold her restaurant and took to the road in a spirited endeavour to redefine the role of the traditional ice-cream van. Morfudd began to experiment with unusual and original flavour combinations – including savoury ingredients, herbs and spices – in order to create delicious home-made ice creams. 'Lola's on Ice' is now arguably the most famous ice-cream van in the country; it has appeared on the television series *Sweet Baby James* with James Martin and continues to provide much entertainment serving up Morfudd's irresistible iced creations at functions and high-profile events.

Lola's
Ice Creams
& Sundaes

Iced delights for all seasons

Morfudd Richards

EBURY
PRESS

To Gillie

1 3 5 7 9 10 8 6 4 2

Published in 2009 by Ebury Press, an imprint of Ebury Publishing

A Random House Group Company

Text copyright © Morfudd Richards 2009

Photography copyright © Ebury Press 2009

The Random House Group Limited Reg. No. 954009 Addresses for companies within the Random House Group can be found at www.randomhouse.co.uk

A CIP catalogue record for this book is available from the British Library

The Random House Group Limited supports The Forest Stewardship Council (FSC), the leading international forest certification organisation. All our titles that are printed on Greenpeace approved FSC certified paper carry the FSC logo. Our paper procurement policy can be found at www.rbooks.co.uk/environment

To buy books by your favourite authors and register for offers visit www.rbooks.co.uk

Printed and bound in England by Butler Tanner and Dennis Ltd

ISBN 9780091926328

Design and photography: Vanessa Courtier

Prop styling: Tessa Evelegh

Contents

Introduction: Finding Mr. Frosty

In 2004 I happened to be looking on eBay, when my eye was caught by a 1970s ice-cream van. It was pink and called Mr. Frosty, and on a whim I bought it. I paid £500 for the van, unseen, and flew down to Cornwall to pick it up, where it was parked in a rundown car park close to Land's End. It was in a filthy state: its windows were covered in peeling lollipop stickers and the freezers were dank and mouldy. I began my return journey to London, but within a hundred miles of leaving Cornwall the engine blew up. Fortunately, I had joined the RAC the previous day, so Mr. Frosty and I got a very comfortable lift home!

Back in London, I joined the Bedford Van Appreciation Society in order to source a replacement engine, drove up to Northamptonshire to pick one up, then found a garage in Hoxton that would fit it. Once mobile again, the van was given a resident's parking permit outside my house in Battersea (to the bemusement of my neighbours), and I set about replacing the interior, holing myself up in its cavernous freezer to remove the fungi feeding on the previous summer's 'whippy' drippings and peeling away the faded stickers from the windows. I hired paint-stripping equipment and patiently burned away the layers of paint on its exterior, hauling in some friends to assist, and then we set to the task of giving Mr. Frosty its new maquillage. It was July and blisteringly hot. As I stood on the roof of my ice-cream van with my hired auto-spray equipment, I could see the paint coagulate in the air before it reached its target.

Eventually the faded pink exterior was replaced with polka dots on the roof and hand-painted psychedelic writing on the front and sides advertising its forthcoming array of flavours – pineapple and chilli sorbet, beetroot and horseradish, Vin Santo ice cream, Poire Belle Hélène and Peach Melba, among others. A visit to a theatrical props shop gave me giant butterflies, which were attached to the outside, while the inside was laden with imitation fruit, vegetables, garlands and box trees. The steering wheel and seat were covered in fake Dalmatian fur, and an imitation owl and peacock were positioned outwards to gaze at curious passers-by. A giant sticker on the front of the van read, 'The ice van cometh'. Although still looking like an old ice-cream van, the transformation from Mr. Frosty to Lola's on Ice was complete!

I hadn't really thought about what I would do with the van when I bought it. I would like to say it was an astute bit of business acumen from an established restaurateur who saw a gap in the market. The truth is really that I just wanted the van! Some sort of vague business plan emerged later, as much from my excitement of driving around in an ice-cream van as anything else. I had never really liked soft-serve ice cream dispensed from a machine or what it represented. Although lighter in fat than custard-based ice cream, its synthetic composition seemed to me the ultimate in dumbing down of the real thing, the diva turned chorus girl, the Pied Piper appearing on a street corner with the jingle of a nursery rhyme...

Today's specials

So I learnt how to make proper ice cream and sorbet. Although I had been running my own restaurant for 10 years, and we had always made our own ices at Lola's, I had only a basic knowledge of ice-cream making. I received enthusiastic advice and ideas from the chefs in my restaurant and read as many recipe books as possible. As my knowledge grew, so too did my confidence. I began to look anew at ingredients and their properties, how they worked together and which savoury ingredients could be successfully made into an ice cream. I wanted to push my own – and other people's – flavour boundaries; to give them something hot, like wasabi, or horseradish, within a 'cold' context, to experiment with textures and their combinations. I had tried Ferran Adrià's food at his restaurant El Bulli in Spain a few months earlier and been blown away by the way he disassembled and re-assembled textures and flavours. The meal was revelatory and inspired in me a desire to apply my own, extremely humble, experiments to my ice-cream flavours. These sorts of ideas were, I think, unchartered territory for an ice-cream van!

I took out Lola's on Ice on a few occasions, wandering the parks and streets of London in search of business – but everywhere I went, I was approached by threatening-looking men making calls on their mobile phones then ordering me to move on. Even though there were no other ice-cream vans to be seen, I was on someone's patch, and I realised I could soon become embroiled in the so-called Ice-cream Wars. One Sunday my friend Delyth and I were moved from Clapham Common, Battersea Park, Brockwell Park and outside Tate Modern, before weaving our way north in exasperation to Sadler's Wells Theatre, where we thought we might try our luck during the matinée interval. Soon a long queue formed from an interval audience delighted to be offered a choice of home-made ice creams and sorbets. A few days later, however, I received a letter from the theatre telling me I was threatening their ice-cream concession stand. I had been 'moved on' again: Mr. Frosty's days on the streets were numbered! So in its new incarnation, I decided it was much safer, and friendlier, to attend private events, taking with me a selection of classic ices plus an expanding collection of more unusual flavours.

Whatever event I am attending with my ice-cream van – a wedding, civil partnership, birthday party or corporate event – I always bring along something extra, an unusual flavour with which to challenge or engage the guests. Beetroot Cassis Sorbet (see page 124) is a favourite for me because of its combination of sweet and savoury, with some people getting the sweetness first followed by earthy flavours or vice versa, and the colour of the sorbet is fabulous! Creamy Horseradish Ice Cream (see page 120) is another tastebud talking point. You may not like horseradish, but you cannot fail to be impressed by the simultaneous shock of hot and cold within its creamy textural context. Ice creams such as Sweet Miso or Roast Red Pepper and Goats' Cheese (see pages 187 and 117) are others that sometimes get added to the list of flavours scribbled on the van's 'Today's Specials'. They always get people talking.

I love driving my van through the streets and watching people's faces break into a smile as they see this slightly beaten-up vehicle covered in huge fake butterflies drive by. And it always gives me pleasure to attend a private event and watch how excited the guests get when they stand in line waiting for their turn, their enthusiasm growing as they near the front of the queue.

Back to basics

This book includes quite a bit about the composition and chemistry of ice cream, which some of you might find useful if you have an interest in the science of ice-cream making. It also features a section on the basics of making ice cream, sorbet,

sherbet and granita. I think we often follow instructions in cookbooks without really understanding why we do things – which steps are vitally important, which are less so, and what corners can be cut, if any. The 'Making Ices' chapter aims to explain why things are done in a particular way – I certainly learnt a great deal from my own research!

When people think of ice cream and sorbet, they generally consider them a summertime treat. Of course, while there is little to match a delectably creamy, fruit-packed ice cream on a hot summer's day, curling up on a winter's evening with a tub of very dark chocolate ice cream is an equally irresistible temptation! For many of us, the association of ice cream is with childhood. I still believe I am that child on Sports Day in Criccieth Primary School, North Wales, wanting to be first to cross the finishing line because the winner got the first cornet of Cadwalader's, the local ice cream. Even now, that's how I see ice cream – as a prize.

Making ice cream and sorbet is great fun, and there is little to match the delights of eating a fresh dollop of something you have whipped up yourself, as it were. It is also really worth experimenting with flavours and their combinations. We usually associate ice cream and sorbet with fruit, but there are many vegetables that can be turned into fabulous ice creams, especially those with an intrinsic sweetness. Suppose you see a tasty and nutritious new crop of carrots in the market. Why not cook them with coriander or orange juice and a little sugar, purée them and combine them with a little cream then churn them in an ice-cream machine and see what happens? Could you make an ice cream from mashed potatoes mixed with crème fraîche and a little caviar spooned in just after churning? So what if your experiments don't work? It will give you a chuckle that you thought they might, and if there are any kids in the house, they can have a good moan and tell you they are feeling deprived or breathe one huge sigh of relief! Ice creams, sorbets, sherbets and granita make great canapés at a party, especially savoury ices. I once took a bunch of canapé-style ices to a group of Welsh friends at the Groucho Club in Soho, and the mix of regular canapés with the iced canapés worked really well. Some people thought my crab ice cream was simply too crabby, while others thought it was delicious. You can't please everyone all the time, but I pleased the opera star Bryn Terfel, and that's not bad! It is always more fun to do things seasonally as well. I won't serve strawberry ice cream from my van in December, for example, because strawberries are not in season. I like the idea of my little van sitting there patiently on its patch of the globe as the planet rotates around the sun, the seasons bringing with them all of their bounty, and my van then setting forth laden with that bounty.

The book also contains a section called 'Sundaes'. I have always regarded a sundae served at a supper party as rather glamorous, in a retro way. Tall sundae glasses heaped with mound upon mound of ice cream, a freshly baked biscuit or fruit on top, and smothered in a rich, glistening sauce. So indulgent. So naughty. There are classic sundaes, as well as combinations of ices based around a theme, which work well when partnered with each other. All of the ices in this section also work as stand-alone recipes. Finally, there is a little bit about this book that is a wink and a nudge. Should you create Welsh Rarebit Ice cream with French Toast (see page 152), for example, I hope you will make it in the spirit in which it was intended, and that your guests will enjoy the joke as much as you do!

1 Composition

What makes up an ice cream?

Really good home-made ice cream is made by achieving a balance of flavour, body and texture. If we use good-quality ingredients and follow a well-thought-out recipe, we will make an ice cream with all these qualities. A recipe is simply a formula, a group of ingredients that interact with each other in a particular way. Understanding how these ingredients relate to each other isn't necessary for making good ice cream, or even for cooking in general, but it does make the process more interesting and may improve our skills in the kitchen.

Increasingly, amateur cooks want to know what processes are occurring when they cook something, and, more importantly, what has happened when it all goes horribly wrong. Gradually the wails of despair over a scrambled custard turn into a reflective sob, then the questions and recriminations begin. Maybe I didn't follow the recipe to the letter, or maybe it was the recipe itself that was at fault! What precisely is going on in the recipe anyway? Is an ice cream made from twelve eggs better than one made from six? And why did I use eggs to make ice cream in the first place? Curiosity over such matters has turned our gaze to science as a way of understanding cooking processes, and it is this understanding that will not only help us to be better cooks but may also bring to our cooking some analytical as well as technical expertise.

But is it enough to make a delicious-tasting ice cream? What if our ice cream is icy or if it lacks body? What has happened if our well-intentioned treat turns out grainy or collapses into a reprehensible mess? Achieving the right texture and body is a little harder than achieving than the right flavour – it requires a balance of the main ingredients and their components, to ensure the correct combination of sweetness, creaminess, ice crystals and air, all of which affect the ice cream's body and texture. If we understand what happens to ice cream as it is being made, and what happens to its components as they interact with each other at the different stages of its production, it will help us to improve the texture and hence the quality of our ice cream.

But first, what exactly is ice cream, apart from a creamy mound of yummy gorgeousness? In technical culinary terms, ice cream is both a foam and an emulsion. A foam is created when gas is dispersed in a liquid; typical foams include foods such as whipped creams, meringues and mousses. The gas in all of these concoctions, as well as in ice cream is, of course, air: the air bubbles are trapped and stabilised within a membrane, made from the fat in the cream and milk. Emulsions are liquid droplets dispersed in other immiscible liquids – that is, liquids that repel each other – they're in bed together, but they're not intimate!

So ice cream is generally made of the following basic elements: milk and/or cream (or a non-dairy alternative); sweeteners; emulsifiers (such as egg yolks); sometimes a stabilising agent (which comes from plant extracts); and finally, and most importantly, the flavouring (such as chocolate or fruit). From these ingredients come their component parts, which in dairy ice cream are milk fat, solids, sweeteners and water. A look at their roles and interaction will really help us to improve the quality of our home-made ice cream.

The fat content of dairy ice cream comes from the milk and cream, but there are also milk-solids-not-fats (known as MSNFs), which come from just the milk. These include solids such as proteins, caseins, salt and lactose (milk sugar). There are also other solids, which come from the sweeteners (that is, sucrose or sucrose substitutes), as well as lecithin and more proteins, which come from egg yolks. There is also water from the egg yolks and the milk (or non-dairy alternative) and, finally, air (which does not come from the ingredients but which is a vital component of ice cream). The composition of ice cream is usually expressed as a percentage of these different components and together these form a complex matrix that, when frozen and churned, gives ice cream its unique characteristics.

Basic components of an ice cream

Dairy milk contains fat, water, salt, vitamins and MSNFs (including proteins, lactose and traces of other compounds). Of these, the fat, lactose and proteins are the most important components, while milk's water content contributes most of the liquid in ice cream that will be converted into ice crystals during the freezing process.

Milk-fat (or butter-fat) is very important for the sensory qualities it brings to ice cream in terms of flavour, texture and colour. It has an unique ability to react with flavour compounds, with the fat content of ice cream affecting its perceived sweetness and intensity of sweetness. Milk-fat also helps give body and viscosity to the ice cream through the process of fat destabilisation (see page 21). The milk-fat content of whole milk in the UK is approximately 4 per cent, although this may vary according to what the cows are fed and the season (cows produce milk with a higher fat content in winter as they approach the end of their lactation period). Guernsey and Jersey cows produce milk rich in fat, which in turn produces very rich ice cream. The fat content of cream varies according to its type. Using cream with a high fat content will not necessarily make for a better ice cream: richer, yes, but too much richness will mask flavour because ice cream with a high fat content has a higher viscosity – this will prevent flavours from reaching the taste receptors in the tongue and palate, and require corresponding increases in sucrose content in order to balance the flavours. Using a cream with a low fat content will prevent a proper fat–air membrane from developing and will result in a hard, icy-textured ice cream.

What proportion of milk to cream should be used when making ice cream? I have looked at lots of recipes in search of the 'perfectly composed ice cream' and it is astonishing how widely they vary. While some cookery writers will use almost twice as much cream in their recipe as milk, others will suggest using little or no cream, in effect making a frozen egg custard.

Some of the recipes in this book fall outside of the 'recommended' ratio guidelines of a 5–20 per cent fat content (including one of my own vanilla ice cream recipes on page 54). They may be considered either too rich or not rich enough, but the point is that you can make ice cream successfully by varying the quantity of ingredients used; disregarding the chemistry behind a dish does not mean it isn't going to satisfy personal preferences.

Milk-solids-not-fats (MSNFs) consist of caseins and other milk proteins, lactose, whey products and minerals. Caseins contribute some emulsifying products to the mix, which help give an ice cream body and 'chew resistance', and assist the ice cream with holding its air. You should always be able to feel the texture of an ice cream on your tongue – if it offers no resistance or simply melts away immediately, it lacks body. Lactose, a carbohydrate, gives milk its sweet taste and helps to supplement the sucrose content. MSNFs, however, have little effect on the flavour of an ice cream and are important more for their contribution to its body and texture. Since lactose makes up over half of MSNFs, too much of these solids in an ice cream will cause the lactose to crystallise and give it a coarse, sandy texture.

Water The water content of ice cream comes primarily from the dairy products used; the remainder comes from the egg yolks. The ice crystals formed by the frozen water are an essential component of an ice cream's structure, but only account for a fraction of its volume. The speed at which ice crystals are formed determines their size and hence whether an ice cream will be smooth or coarse: the faster the rate of freezing, the smaller the ice crystals. The smaller the ice crystals, the smoother the ice cream, so it is important to ensure a rapid freezing of the ice-cream mix in order to obtain a plethora of small seed crystals that will be distributed evenly throughout the mix through the churning action. Large ice crystals should be avoided because they coarsen the texture.

Sweeteners

Sweetness is one of just five tastes that the human tongue can detect and is a primary component of ice cream. Human beings have taste receptors that register the presence of sugars and attach to them the sensation of pleasure because it is the brain's way of ensuring that we get the energy that fuels our cells. There are various sweetening agents that can be used to make ice cream, and these are sometimes used alone or in combination with each other because they each have distinctive properties and sweetening capacities; their use is required not only as a flavouring agent but also as a preservative, as a humectant (moisture retaining substance), to give body to the ice cream and to improve its textural properties.

Sucrose is the scientific name for what we commonly call sugar and is the most frequently used sweetener in ice cream. It not only sweetens ice cream but also gives body and improves viscosity by increasing the total solid content. Green plants produce sucrose during photosynthesis whereas human beings obtain it industrially from sugar cane and sugar beets.

Sucrose not only enhances flavour, but also lowers the freezing point of a solution. As water freezes out of a solution, it doesn't take the sugar molecules with it and leaves them behind as a very concentrated solution. This process is what prevents ice cream from freezing into a solid block of ice and makes it scoopable at subzero temperatures.

Glucose syrup known in the United States as corn syrup, is a purified aqueous solution of nutritive saccharides obtained from starch. It is produced in the same way that we break down starch in our digestive systems, through acids and enzymes. The starch, extracted from apples, potatoes, corn, rice and so on, if entirely broken down, produces individual glucose molecules. These molecules are highly viscous and inhibit the formation of large ice crystals, because they coat the seed crystals formed during the freezing process and prevent them from attaching to each other to make larger crystals.

Many of the ice cream and sorbet recipes in this book include the option of adding glucose syrup to the mix; I use it regularly because it contributes a firmer and chewier texture to the ice cream and prevents the crystallisation of sucrose, so it makes the ices smoother. Glucose syrup also gives more 'length' to the sensation of sweetness in the ice cream than sucrose. Different sugars give different impressions of sweetness. Sucrose is not detected immediately but has a lingering sweetness. Glucose syrup is not detected immediately either, and it does not have the same intensity as sucrose, but remains on the palate for longer. It also lowers the freezing point of ice cream; because it takes longer to freeze, the ice cream will be softer.

Glucose syrup has less than half the sweetening capacity of sucrose, although, for the sake of practicality, I have regarded glucose syrup as being half as sweet as sugar. If you are using the recipes in this book, you can choose either a combination of sucrose and glucose syrup or sucrose alone. Glucose syrup is available in most larger supermarkets, grocer's or kitchen and cookware shops, albeit in small quantities of about 100 g.

Emulsifiers are a group of compounds that, when added to an ice-cream mix, assist in the development of its fat structure and air distribution in order to enrich its body and texture and give good melt-down. While there are a number of emulsifiers available for commercial use, the recipes in this book use only egg yolk as an emulsifying agent.

Egg yolks The yolk of an egg contains water, iron, vitamin A and proteins, including lecithin, a natural emulsifier. Each lecithin molecule contains a water-loving portion and a fat-loving portion, which means that it acts as a bridging agent between the two incompatible liquids (think marriage counsellor). Once the custard base for an ice cream is cooked, the emulsifiers displace the proteins coating the fat droplets. The fat droplets are then destabilised by being knocked about by the paddles during churning but the lecithin enables the fat–water liquid to coalesce.

The 'graininess' that can sometimes be felt on an ice cream made without emulsifiers is due to the fact that the fat droplets are still encased in a protein coating and have resisted partially merging with each other. Instead, they remain as individual fat droplets within the ice cream, hence the perception of graininess on the tongue.

Emulsifiers also control the melt-down rate of an ice cream. When an ice cream is, for example, scooped into a bowl or cone, the ice crystals start to melt and the foam structure begins to collapse. However, even after the ice crystals have melted, the ice cream itself does not collapse until the fat-stabilised foam structure also collapses; the rate at which the ice cream begins to topple is inhibited by the use of emulsifiers.

Some styles of ice cream, such as the Philadelphia style (see page 242), are made without the use of egg yolk and simply combine milk and/or cream with sugar and a flavouring. Although the casein proteins in milk and cream do have some emulsifying properties, this style of ice cream is likely to be grainier due to the reasons stated earlier. However, I often use the Philadelphia style for making ice cream because it is quick and appeals to those not wanting to eat eggs.

Air pockets are trapped in the ice-cream mix when it is churned during the freezing process. They are held in suspension by the matrix of ice crystals and destabilised fat, making the foam/emulsion lighter. The more air there is in an ice cream, the 'warmer' it will feel on the palate. The trapped air inflates the volume of the original mix, and this increase is called 'overrun'. The denser the ice cream, the lower the overrun will be.

How the components interact

You begin making ice cream by pasteurising and homogenising it. That is, you combine the milk and/or cream with the sugar (and egg yolks, if using), heat the custard up to the pasteurisation temperature of 79.4°C for 15 seconds (to destroy any potentially harmful bacteria), and then rapidly cool it. Homogenisation occurs during the heating process – the fat droplets from the milk and cream begin to break down into similarly sized small droplets coated in milk proteins that are adsorbed or held to the surface of the fat droplets (that is, they coat the surface as opposed to being absorbed, or swallowed up, into the fat). Ice cream is smooth if everything in it is small – the fat droplets, the solids, the air and the ice crystals.

The custard is then rapidly cooled and the emulsifiers (in our case egg yolks) adsorb to the surface of the fat droplets, replacing some of the milk proteins on the surface. The ice cream is then allowed to mature, or rest, so that the melted fat droplets begin to re-crystallise. They will not fully re-crystallise because there are other things in the mix, like water, sucrose and egg yolks (or an alternative emulsifier), but this partial re-crystallisation is an important step in improving the texture of the ice cream. Essentially, the fat has been broken down during heating and mixed in with other components and is now re-forming in a different way.

The custard is then churned either in an ice-cream machine or by the 'still-freezing' method (see page 43). At this point the fat droplets in the custard will begin partially to break down and de-stabilise again because the paddle in the ice-cream machine is knocking them about. The fat droplets are 'unstable' because the coating from the emulsifiers is weaker than the original protein coating from the milk proteins – thus the fat droplets have less resistance to the action of the churning paddles that causes them to collide with each other. This is a good thing and the whole point of using egg yolks or other emulsifiers! If emulsifiers were not added, the fat droplets would resist flocculation (forming into clumps) due to the strong protein coating on their surface. By adding emulsifiers, the fat droplets become partially liquid and partially solid, and form clusters while still retaining their individual identity.

The air bubbles being whipped into the custard through the churning process are then 'held together' by this partially coalesced fat that is acting like a membrane to trap the air. The process is the same as if you were whipping cream. If ice cream is 'over-whipped', the fat droplets will break down completely and turn to butter.

In the meantime, another drama is unfolding. The water content of the ice-cream mix is being frozen, creating ice crystals, which also gives ice cream its structure. The water in the mix contains broken-down sugars, but when the water begins to freeze into ice crystals, it freezes in its pure form, leaving the sugars behind. So water, when frozen, will literally migrate away from anything dissolved in it (issues with commitment, maybe?). As more and more ice crystals form, the sugar solution left behind becomes increasingly concentrated. Water freezes at 0°C, but when sugar is added to it, the freezing point is lowered. As the sugar solution increases in concentration, this in turn lowers the freezing point even further. This process continues to very low temperatures and is called 'freezing point depression'.

Only about three-quarters of the water in an ice cream ever freezes (the other quarter remains a very concentrated sugar solution), which is why it is possible to scoop ice cream at subzero temperatures and why it is chewable.

Alternatives to dairy

For those who have an aversion to or intolerance of dairy products, there are alternative milks available that can be used to make ice cream.

Goats' milk contains smaller chain fatty-acids and marginally less lactose than cows' milk and is often regarded as being easier to digest. The fat content of goats' milk is approximately the same as cows' milk, though, unlike cows' milk, goats' milk is naturally homogenised (which means the cream remains suspended in the milk, instead of rising to the top). The same is true of sheep's milk. Goats' milk has a tangier, more distinctive flavour than milk from other animals.

Sheep's milk has a higher fat content than cows' milk, approximately 6.9–7.5 per cent (cows' milk is 3.6–5.2 per cent, depending on the breed), and contains more non-fat solids than cows' milk. Sheep's milk has the second-highest level of calcium after buffalo milk. Sheep, like goats and water buffalo, process almost all the carotene from green feed, so that their milk is completely white (Guernsey and Jersey cows, on the other hand, convert very little carotene and produce golden milk). Sheep's milk has a sweet, slightly nutty flavour; it is milder than goats' milk but has a stronger flavour than cows' milk.

Water-buffalo milk also has a higher content of butter-fat and non-fat solids than cows' milk, approximately 6.9 per cent. It lacks the yellow pigment carotene found in cows' milk, which is why it can be made into pure white cheeses, such as mozzarella. Water-buffalo milk is also higher in lactose than cows' milk, but some find it easier to digest, possibly because its protein structure is different from cows' milk.

Buffalo milk is reputed to have a lower cholesterol level than cows', goats' or sheep's milk and the highest calcium level of the three. It has a similar flavour to cows' milk.

Soya milk is made by soaking soybeans until they are soft and grinding them with water. This results in a liquid filled with soy proteins and tiny droplets of soy oil. Soya milk contains a lower fat content than cows' milk, approximately 2 per cent, and about the same amount of protein as cows' milk. The fat, however, is less saturated.

Ice cream made from soya milk is a good vegan alternative to ice cream made from animal products and excellent flavours can be obtained if it is combined with other ingredients such as fruit purées or chocolate. However, because it has such a low fat content, it is difficult to obtain very good textural qualities and can sometimes be icy. Adding glucose syrup will help to prevent this.

2 Flavours

Try these at home

The list of flavours that can feature in ice creams, sorbets, sherbets and granitas is endless, and I have always championed experimenting with whatever flavour takes your fancy. However, I am going to concentrate here on some of the most common ones. I have also included a little bit more information about the main ingredients, such as milk, cream and sugar. They are not flavours as such, but they do add flavour, and so I felt they merited inclusion.

Alcohol may provide its own flavour but can also be used to heighten or intensify another flavour – for example vodka added to chocolate, or kirsch added to fruit purées. Alcohol has a very low freezing point so it prevents ices from freezing too hard and makes them softer.

Care should be taken, though: too much alcohol prevents the ice cream or sorbet from freezing at all, or else causes them to collapse easily once they start to soften. This is especially true of sorbets, which do not have the 'fat structure' of an ice cream within which to hold the alcohol.

Chocolate comes from the cocoa tree as a pod that contains lots of rows of small, fleshy white fruit. The cocoa bean is essentially the seed germ of the fruit, and there are three main varieties. Criollo beans are generally regarded as having the highest quality but are low yielding, representing only 10–15 per cent of the world's production, and are prone to disease. They have a fruity, slightly acid flavour. Forastero beans are mainly grown in Africa and Brazil, and are more robust and higher yielding but do not have the flavour complexities of the Criollo and are used either for blending or on their own. However, like any crop, cocoa is affected by the vagaries of 'terroir', the French word commonly used to describe the physical and environmental characteristics of a site, and a Forastero grown and fermented under ideal conditions may be superior to a Criollo grown and fermented under poor conditions. The Trinitario bean is a hybrid of the two and is mainly used for blending.

Most chocolate sold indicates the percentage of cocoa solids on the label, and many recipe books suggest using chocolate with a particular 'minimum cocoa content'. This means the entire cocoa content, i.e. the cocoa bean's mass, or solids, and the cocoa butter (the fat from the bean). However, the percentage shown does not tell you the precise proportion of cocoa solids and cocoa butter (during processing the cocoa mass is separated from the cocoa butter), so two different chocolate bars indicating the same percentage of combined cocoa solids and butter may be completely different from each other. To complicate matters, percentage of cocoa solids is no indication of the quality and origin of the cocoa beans themselves.

For the ice-cream maker in search of top-quality chocolate, what all this means is that because the quality and flavour of the chocolate available to us can vary so much, it is really worth trying out a few of the estate-sourced chocolates and different brands to see which ones you prefer. I generally use chocolate with a minimum cocoa solids content of 70 per cent. A 'chocolate tasting' is lots of fun, especially if you get everyone to concentrate and make tasting notes!

White chocolate is made of pure cocoa butter, milk solids, sugar and flavouring. Since some brands of white chocolate contain cocoa-butter substitutes, such as vegetable oil, you should check that the ingredients list on the packet actually specifies cocoa butter.

Cocoa powder comes from the ground-up bean kernel once the cocoa butter has been removed, although some cocoa butter remains. It then undergoes a process known as 'dutching', which removes the acidity. Adding cocoa powder to chocolate ice cream or sorbet will intensify the flavour, but you could also make a chocolate sorbet using just cocoa powder, water and sugar. When buying cocoa powder, make sure it is not sweetened. It is quite different from drinking chocolate, which has sugar, and possibly other ingredients, added to it.

Cream The minimum fat content of cream is generally 55 per cent in clotted cream, 48 per cent in double cream, 35 per cent in whipping cream, and 18 per cent in single cream.

I use whipping cream in most (but not all) of my recipes because it provides the right balance of texture and flavour when combined with other ingredients. Of course, the use of clotted or double cream gives you a much richer ice cream, but sometimes too much butter-fat masks the flavours of the other ingredients. If you use a cream with too little fat, such as single cream, it gives you a lighter ice cream, but one that may turn out icy. Many gelato recipes use little or no cream, which makes the ice cream denser and less rich. If you cannot find whipping cream, buy double cream and dilute it with whole milk (replacing approximately a third of the double cream with whole milk).

Soured cream and crème fraîche were traditionally made by letting fresh cream turn sour naturally, as the bacteria in the cream both fermented and thickened it. Today, they are made by introducing bacterial cultures to pasteurised cream until it sours and thickens, then re-pasteurising it to halt the process.

Crème fraîche has a minimum fat content of approximately 30 per cent, while that of soured cream is approximately 20 per cent. Both can be used to make ice cream and sherbet, but I prefer to use crème fraîche as an alternative to regular cream because of its richer, more distinctively tangy flavour.

Eggs For ethical and quality reasons, I have a preference for organic eggs or eggs sourced directly from farmers' markets or at the farm gate. Farmers who are concerned about hen welfare are also likely to have fed their flock a balanced diet, which means the eggs have a better flavour.

Fruit Different types of fruit perform differently when added to ice cream or made into sorbet, according to their sugar:water ratio. Limes, for example, have a sugar content of 2 per cent while dates are 65 per cent sugar. Some fruits, such as blueberries and pineapples, have a high pectin content, which will make the ice cream or sorbet firmer or chewier.

Always try and keep to seasonal produce if you can as it has the best flavour, and discard any damaged fruit. If you choose to buy organic fruit, you will know that they have not been sprayed with pesticides. You can find good-quality frozen berries or freeze the berries yourself and use them later in the season; there are also various good-quality fruit purées to be found, but bear in mind that some have sugar already added – check the ingredients list carefully and adjust the recipe accordingly.

Herbs Avoid using dried herbs in ices as they do not impart their flavour in the same way as fresh herbs and can leave a 'woody' after-taste. Fresh herbs need to be infused for approximately 15 minutes to release their flavours.

Honey is a mixture of glucose, fructose and sucrose that bees produce from plant nectar. Honey contains nearly 20 per cent water as well as traces of acids, vitamins, minerals and enzymes. It is sweeter than sucrose because it is primarily fructose and glucose, and it has similar characteristics and qualities to invert sugar (see Questions & Answers, page 246). The flavour and colour of honey is dependent upon the types of flowers from which the bees gather the nectar; each has its own flavour profile. Honey is used in ice-cream making for the various flavourings it brings and not generally as a companion or alternative to sucrose.

Milk I use whole milk with a minimum fat content of approximately 4 per cent whenever a recipe includes milk. You may, of course, substitute semi-skimmed milk, but bear in mind that the reduced-fat option alters the texture of the ice cream. Skimmed milk should not, generally, be used as it really makes the ice cream too icy. I prefer to use Soil Association-certified milk from organically reared cattle because of its strict standards on animal welfare.

Avoid condensed milk, which is too sweet, unless your are making kulfi, the Indian style ice cream, and also avoid UHT or 'long life' milks, which have been heated to a high temperature and do not have the same flavour profile as fresh milk.

Nuts are very versatile and can be either added directly to an ice cream to give it a crunchy texture or made into a praline and used as a topping. The flavour of nuts is heightened if you dry roast them in the oven for a few minutes. Nuts have a high oil content so ensure that any nuts you use are fresh since they rapidly lose their flavour and can go rancid – pretty horrible! Store nuts in a dark, cool place and in a sealed container. I sometimes place them in freezer bags and freeze them, but for no longer than a month.

Spices Be judicious in your use of spices as they can overwhelm other flavours. Spices should be infused in heated milk, or non-dairy equivalent, for 15–30 minutes. The most important test, of course, is to taste as you go along. Spices diminish in flavour and aroma if left around for too long, and are inexpensive to replace regularly. Make sure that you buy your spices from shops that have a high stock turnover.

Sugar The primary sugar suggested in the recipes in this book is caster sugar, but you can substitute granulated sugar since the heating of the sucrose in solution ensures the crystals are fully dissolved. I prefer to use caster sugar for the simple reason that it is more versatile than granulated sugar and is available at all times in my kitchen for baking as well as for making ice cream. Do not use icing sugar as it has other things added to it.

Unrefined sugars such as demerara and muscovado should not be used instead of caster sugar, unless a recipe specifies it. Such sugars have flavours that are stronger and richer than granulated and caster sugars; they result in a different end product.

Vanilla is the second most costly spice after saffron and is revered for its aromatic pungency and depth and richness of flavour. Vanilla comes from the cured pods of the orchid Vanilla planifolia, a tropical plant that is indigenous to the New World and was first used by the Aztecs to flavour their chocolate drinks.

The different vanilla species produce different flavour profiles. Bourbon vanilla from Madagascar is regarded as having the richest flavour. Indonesian vanilla pods have smoky qualities and a lighter note of vanillin. Mexican pods have a distinctive fruity aroma and do not contain the plethora of seeds of Bourbon pods. Tahitian vanilla has a more subtle flavour than Bourbon pods and is more perfumed and flowery.

Both the vanilla seeds and the pod can be used in flavouring ice cream. The pod can be opened lengthways with a knife, and its sticky resinous material, in which the seeds are embedded, scraped out and used. The pod itself, once emptied, still retains flavour compounds and may be added to sugar to make vanilla sugar or soaked for approximately half an hour in a warm liquid to extract its flavour.

Look out for vanilla extract if you cannot obtain vanilla pods. It is obtained by immersing the pods in alcohol and water for a period of days then ageing it to extract the flavour. However, vanilla extract will not give you the depth of flavour and aromatics of the vanilla bean. Avoid vanilla essence, which is manufactured synthetically and does not have the depth of flavour of real vanilla.

Yoghurt is produced by the bacterial fermentation of milk. Anyone with lactose intolerance may safely eat it because the fermentation process converts most of the lactose in milk to lactic acid, which is what provides yoghurt's characteristic sour taste. Yoghurt can be made not only from cows' milk but also from most animals that produce milk, as well as from soya milk.

Greek yoghurt has a fat content of 10 per cent and a tangy flavour profile that complements many fruits, vegetables and spices. I use it regularly as a low-fat alternative to cream. Yoghurts with a fat content lower than 10 per cent may produce an icy-textured ice cream.

3 Making ices

Ice cream

There are two ways of making ice cream: the Philadelphia method (see page 242) and the traditional method. Philadelphia-style ice cream is made simply by combining a fruit or flavouring with milk and/or cream and sugar then churning it in an ice-cream machine or by the still-freezing method (see page 43). This is an easy and handy way to make ice cream in a hurry. However, if you wish to make ice cream by the traditional method, you have to make a custard infused with a flavour (such as vanilla) or add the flavour (say strawberry) later. This procedure is more time-consuming but ensures that your ice cream gets real depth of flavour and a proper texture. Since making ice cream is as much about achieving the right body and texture as it is about intensity of flavour, I prefer to use the traditional method, although the Philadelphia style no doubt has its merits, primarily speed and simplicity.

Having said that, it really is not difficult making ice cream by the traditional method, even if it does requires a little practice and patience! This chapter deals with how to make ice cream by the traditional method. It does not take into account individual recipe variations.

How to make ice cream: the principles

1 Heat the milk (or non-dairy equivalent) and/or cream in a heavy-duty pan. Use a non-reactive pan made from stainless steel or anodised aluminium. The liquid should be heated till bubbles appear around the edge of the pan and it is hot enough to enable any flavourings to be infused and glucose syrup, if using, to dissolve.

You may wish to add the cream after the custard has been made as it speeds up the cooling process. However, it is better to heat the milk and cream at the same time as it breaks down the fat droplets and makes them less likely to clump together. This is the first part in the process of creating a fat structure – a mass of tiny fat droplets that eventually become a partial membrane capable of trapping the air churned into it.

2 If the recipe calls for fresh herbs or spices, these should be added to the pan along with the milk and cream, and allowed to infuse.

3 If the recipe does not include egg yolks, then the sugar should also be added to the milk and heated so that it fully dissolves.

4 If the recipe does include egg yolks, these can be combined with the sugar and whisked together. It is easier to separate the egg yolks from their whites if the eggs are cold so keep them in the fridge. You may ask, why bother whisking the sugar with the egg yolks? Why not stick the sugar in with the milk and/or cream until it dissolves then whisk the egg yolks on their own? This is purely a matter of choice, since it appears there is no difference between combining the eggs with the sugar and whipping them up together and dissolving the sugar in the warmed milk–cream mix and whipping the eggs up on their own. I prefer the former since combining the sugar with the eggs may give the eggs more stability when they are being tempered with the milk and cream, but this is purely speculation.

If you decide to whisk the egg yolks with the sugar, you do not need to do so until they are pale yellow and doubled in volume (as you would do for baking) as any air incorporated into the mix will be lost during cooking. Simply whisk the eggs and sugar together until they are combined.

5 The warm milk–cream and egg–sugar mix are then combined. If you add the egg–sugar mixture directly into the warm milk, the eggs will start cooking before they mix thoroughly with the milk, and they will scramble. You must, therefore, temper the egg–sugar mix by adding the warm milk to it a little at a time and whisking constantly before returning the mix to the pan. These ingredients combine to form the base of the custard that can then be cooked on a direct heat.

6 Many recipe books suggest that the custard is placed in a heatproof bowl set over a pan of simmering water, or a bain-marie, in order to avoid scrambling the custard due to direct contact with the heat. However, the custard can be cooked perfectly safely so long as it is kept on a moderate heat, stirred continuously, preferably with a whisk or spatula, and never left alone – not even for a few seconds.

As you cook the custard, make sure you scrape the bottom of the pan while you are stirring so that you avoid any 'eggy' bits coagulating. The custard should be gradually brought up to a temperature of not less than 79.4°C and held at this temperature for 15 seconds in order to pasteurise it and destroy pathogenic bacteria. All of the custard-based recipes in this book are heated to 80°C, so you are well within the limits of safety.

If you don't have a probe thermometer (see page 238), a traditional method of checking if a custard has cooked is by seeing if it has thickened sufficiently to coat the back of a spoon. If you then draw a line with your finger across the back of the spoon and a clear line forms, the custard is cooked. If the line starts to disappear very quickly, it means the custard needs more cooking. However, I do not find this method to be very reliable as the custard can appear cooked before it has actually been pasteurised (a probe thermometer will verify this). It is generally safer, therefore, to use a probe thermometer.

Once the optimum temperature has been reached, it is important to turn off the heat immediately and to continue stirring the custard for a few minutes – this prevents any unwanted increase in temperature and reduces the possibility of the custard curdling. You really do not want to boil your custard, as you will find yourself with a pan full of scrambled eggs!

7 Once the custard is cooked, it must be cooled as rapidly as possible to a temperature of 4°C over a period of $1^{1}/_{2}$ hours and kept at that temperature until it is churned.

The reason that the custard should be cooled quickly is because bacteria can grow most rapidly at human blood temperature, so this critical period should be passed through as quickly as possible. Once cooked, transfer the custard to a container and place it in an ice bath: ice cubes and cold water placed in either a large shallow container or the kitchen sink. I often use frozen ice packs straight from the freezer in lieu of ice cubes. You may need to replace the iced water several times during the cooling process, and if you have made a large quantity of custard, split the contents among several containers as smaller amounts cool quicker. Stir the custard at regular intervals as this helps it to cool.

8 Once the custard has cooled to the required temperature, it is then covered and kept in the fridge at a temperature of 4°C for a minimum of 4 hours in order to mature or rest. Hervé This, in his book *Kitchen Mysteries*, points out that, surprisingly, hot water freezes more rapidly than cold water, so why not put the freshly cooked custard directly into the ice-cream machine? After all, this would cool it rapidly, thus avoiding any danger of bacterial growth and avoiding all of the bother of ice baths and waiting around. You would, however, be omitting a vital step in the ice-cream making process. Allowing the custard to rest enables the fat droplets to crystallise, and this improves the ice cream's texture and viscocity. Studies have shown that it takes at least 4 hours for fat crystallisation to complete in an ice-cream mix. (Think how long it takes for melted butter to crystallise once it is put in the fridge.) This waiting period also enhances flavour development. When I make ice cream, I think of it as a two-day process – I make the custard on the first day and then put it in a covered container and leave it in the fridge overnight to rest before churning it the following day.

9 After resting for the required period, the ice cream is ready to be churned either in an ice-cream machine, according to the manufacturer's instructions, or by hand, using the 'still-freezing' method (see page 43).

10 Once the ice cream is churned, transfer it to a sealed container. The top of the ice cream should be covered with waxed or greaseproof paper to prevent shrinkage. Shrinkage is caused by a loss of air bubbles and, to some degree, by a loss of moisture that, perhaps surprisingly, escapes from frozen products once they are put in the freezer; so it is important to ensure it is minimised.

11 Even after churning the ice cream until firm, it is not actually ready to be eaten (although I often do) and, ideally, should undergo the final 'hardening' process. About 40 per cent of the water that can be frozen within the ice cream remains unfrozen even after churning. Putting the ice cream in the freezer will enable the remaining water to freeze into small ice crystals, giving the ice cream a 'chewable' texture that is absent when it has just been churned. You should try to freeze the ice cream as quickly as possible to avoid the growth of large ice crystals. If your freezer has adjustable settings, set it as cold as possible in advance of making the ice cream and place the ice cream in the coldest part of the freezer to encourage rapid hardening.

While the procedure for hardening ice cream is correct, having already followed the quite lengthy processes of making ice cream, it may seem frustrating then to have to wait even longer before you can eat it! So I have simply said, transfer the ice cream to the freezer until needed without specifying the amount of time it should remain there (which is difficult to assess in any case as it is not only recipe dependent but also depends on the temperature of your freezer. I generally leave the ice cream to harden for at least three hours if possible.) However, should you wish to serve the ice cream straight away, that is fine; if any corner can be cut, it is this one.

12 Once the ice cream has hardened in the freezer, all the ice crystals are now small and of a uniform size, and the ice cream is the right consistency. However, you may find that your ice cream is too hard to eat!

So, you must now bring it up to serving temperature by letting it soften. This may take up to an hour, depending on the recipe and the temperature of your freezer. Ice creams with alcohol and caramel are generally soft enough to scoop almost immediately. The ideal temperature for serving ice cream is approximately −5°C to −7°C.

Sorbet, sherbet and granita

A sorbet is a water-based ice containing no dairy products, though it may sometimes includes a raw egg white. The French term *sorbet* or 'water ice' comes from the Italian *sorbetto*, from their verb *sorbire*, meaning 'to sip', which is in turn a derivation of *sharab*, the Arabic term for a sweetened drink.

The word sherbet now has a variety of meanings, one of which is a water-based ice containing milk.

A granita is a still-frozen, coarse-textured water ice originating from Sicily, where it is often eaten with brioche for breakfast in the summer. Both sorbet and granita are made using sugar, water and flavouring – primarily, but not exclusively, fruit purées and juices – but their textures and the way they are made are different. Sorbets are churned in an ice-cream machine or by the 'still-freezing' method to whip air into them and produce tiny ice crystals of uniform, smooth texture. Granitas are never churned and are always 'still-frozen'. They are dense and coarse-textured – 'butch' sorbets, if you like.

The texture of sorbet and sherbet varies according to the recipe and the temperature at which they are served. Granita requires less sugar than sorbet or sherbet; sorbet and sherbet require sufficient sugar to create a syrup, which, together with any fruit purée, coats the ice crystals formed during freezing and churning, making the texture softer and more palatable. However, some fruits have more natural sugar than others, and these require less added sugar. Generally, if you were to purée fruit and churn it without adding a stock syrup (see below), the ratio of water, sugar and broken-down fruit pulp would be incorrect. You need sufficient water in the mix to form into tiny ice crystals for a smooth consistency.

Stock syrup Stock syrup (also known as sugar syrup or simple syrup) is a mixture of sugar and water brought to the boil and then sometimes simmered for a period to reduce it, depending on the recipe. Making sorbet and granita successfully requires getting the right quantities of sugar and water – not so easy if you don't know how much water and sugar already exists in the puréed fruit or any other flavourings (such as alcohol). Stock syrup is measured by density of sugar, using a hydrometer or saccharometer, and calculated in degrees Baumé. So, 1 kg of sugar with 1 litre of water will yield a simple syrup that is 28 degrees Baumé. This is generally regarded as the best stock syrup for making sorbet; it can then have its sugar density reduced, if making granita, by the addition of water.

I have always used a 28-degree Baumé syrup and have never owned a saccharometer. I have, however, used the tried-and-trusted egg test, since I am never without the odd egg hanging around in my kitchen. Take a fresh egg, wash and dry it, and pop it into the pre-churned sorbet mix. If the egg floats near the top, with only a little of the shell visible above the surface, the mix has the correct sugar:water ratio. If the egg is floating too buoyantly above the surface, there is too much sugar in the mix; if the egg is nowhere to be seen, it will need its sugar level increased.

If you wish to make denser stock syrup, simmer the syrup and watch its viscosity increase. Conversely, if you add water to the stock syrup, you lower its density. When making granita, stock syrup with a Baumé degree of 8–10 is generally recommended. This is achieved by adding approximately three times the quantity of water to stock syrup.

Always make stock syrup first, before beginning a sorbet or granita, unless the primary ingredient needs some level of cooking in a water–sugar mix. It is useful to have it at hand in the fridge – for pouring over a simple fruit salad, for example – but, more importantly, if you are making sorbet or granita on a regular basis, it saves you the bother of having to prepare a stock syrup on every occasion.

Don't let all this talk of sugar density put you off making sorbet, sherbet or granita. They are incredibly easy and fun to make and do not require pasteurisation and rapid cooling as ice creams do, although a short period for flavour development is still recommended. Sorbets and granitas are also perfect for vegans or those with an intolerance of, or allergy to, animal products. You will notice that under the fruit recipe section (see pages 78–111) there are many sorbets. With crops of fruit so ripe and abundant, why not taste them in as pure and simple a form as possible?

How to make sorbet and sherbet: the principles

1 Make a simple stock syrup according to the recipe (see page 49).

2 Combine the stock syrup with the glucose syrup (if using) and heat, stirring, until the glucose syrup has dissolved. I replace part of the sugar quantity with glucose syrup most of the time when I am making a sorbet or a sherbet because it makes them smoother. It has also less than half the sweetening capacity of sucrose.

Glucose syrup, like treacle, is not particularly easy to handle, because it is so viscous and sticky. It is also difficult to weigh to exact proportions. As a general rule, one tablespoon of glucose syrup is approximately 30–40 g.

3 If the recipe calls for any fresh herbs or spices to be infused, these should be added to the pan along with stock syrup. The period for which an ingredient should infuse depends whether it is fresh or dried (see Questions & Answers, page 242). The best test is to taste everything as you go along.

4 Combine the stock syrup with the flavouring. The flavouring for a sorbet or sherbet is generally fruit, alcohol, chocolate, herbs, spices and/or possibly a vegetable. Alcohol will lower the freezing point of the mix, as will salt, even a pinch of it.

5 The mix may then be placed in a covered container and left in the fridge for a couple of hours to allow the flavours to develop. This step is not absolutely crucial; if you are short of time, it can be skipped.

6 Churn the sorbet or sherbet in an ice-cream machine according to the manufacturer's instructions. Do not over-churn it as too much air will make the sorbet 'fluffy', and it will have the consistency more of compressed snow than frozen water ice.

If you do not have an ice-cream machine, you can churn the sorbet or sherbet by hand using the 'still-freezing' method that follows:

Place the mix into a sealed container and put it into the coldest part of the freezer. After 1–1$^{1}/_{2}$ hours, remove the container from the freezer and beat the mix with either a fork or an electric whisk in order to make a uniform slush. Return the mixture to the freezer and repeat this process twice at intervals of 1–1$^{1}/_{2}$ hours. After it has been beaten three times, return it to the freezer for a further hour or so and it should then be ready to serve.

The principles of making sorbet or sherbet according to this method are the same as if making them in an ice-cream machine. Beating the mix with a fork does two things – it creates a plethora of small ice crystals of uniform consistency, and it beats air into the mix so that it is a whipped frozen ice as opposed to a solid block of frozen ice.

The disadvantage of the 'still-freezing' method is that it requires more work than putting the mix into an ice-cream machine and it is harder to achieve a light, smooth product.

7 If you are not serving the sorbet immediately, cover the top of the sorbet with waxed or greaseproof paper to protect it from shrinkage and put it in a sealed container in the freezer.

8 Even after churning the sorbet or sherbet until firm, it is not actually ready to be eaten (although I often do) and still should undergo the final 'hardening' process (see ice-cream hardening, page 38).

9 Once the sorbet or sherbet has hardened in the freezer, all the ice crystals are small and of a uniform size and the right consistency. However, you may now find that it is too hard to eat!

So once hardened, it must be allowed to soften at room temperature. This may take up to an hour, depending on the recipe and the temperature at which it was kept in the freezer.

Allowing a sorbet or sherbet to soften, and thus partially melt, produces a softer, smoother product; those containing alcohol will soften at a faster rate. The ideal temperature for serving sorbet and sherbet is approximately $-5°C$ to $-7°C$, but again this depends on the recipe.

Making granita: the principles

1 Make a simple stock syrup according to the recipe on page 49.

2 If the recipe calls for any fresh herbs or spices to be infused, these should be added to the pan along with the stock syrup. The period for which an ingredient should infuse is dependent upon the product itself, and whether it is fresh or dried (see Questions & Answers, page 242). The best test is to taste everything as you go along.

3 Combine the stock syrup with the flavouring. The flavouring for a granita is generally fruit, alcohol, chocolate, herbs, spices and possibly a vegetable. Alcohol will lower the freezing point of the mix, as will salt, even a pinch of it.

4 Granitas contain less sugar than sorbets or sherbets, in order to maintain their coarse texture. Adding water to the mix decreases the density of the pre-prepared stock syrup. Sometimes cooks add gelatine to a granita mix to maintain a firm crystal structure.

5 The mix can then be placed in a covered container and put it in the fridge for a couple of hours to allow the flavours to develop. This step is not absolutely crucial, and if you are short of time, it can be skipped.

6 To freeze a granita, place the mix in a shallow sealed container and place it in the coldest part of the freezer. It is easier to scrape the ice crystals together in a shallow container than a deep one. Check it after an hour. If it has started to freeze around the edges, scrape the frozen crystals with a fork and combine them with the remaining liquid. Return the container to the freezer and then check it every 30 minutes or so, scraping the frozen crystals from the sides and stirring them together. After 2–2$^{1}/_{2}$ hours you will have a uniform texture of rough frozen crystals.

4 Recipes

Notes on the recipes

Butter All butter is unsalted.

Chocolate I have a preference for chocolate that has a minimum of 70 per cent cocoa solids because of the intensity and complexity of flavour. With white chocolate you should always check that the ingredients list on the packet specifies cocoa butter (and not a substitute such as vegetable oil). For more information about choosing chocolate, see page 26.

Cream I use whipping cream in most, but not all, of my recipes because it provides the right balance of texture and flavour when combined with other ingredients. If you cannot find whipping cream, buy double cream and dilute it with whole milk (replacing approximately a third of the double cream with whole milk).

Eggs If a recipe calls for eggs, it refers to large eggs with the yolks weighing approximately 19–21 g.

Milk If a recipe specifies milk, use whole cows' milk (with a minimum fat content of approximately 4 per cent), unless otherwise advised. You may, of course, instead use semi-skimmed milk, but bear in mind that the reduced-fat option alters the texture of the ice cream.

Serving sizes assume that each serving will be a double scoop. A double scoop is approximately 150 g. Canapé portions are 20–40 g or 1–2 heaped tbsp.

Sugar The primary sugar suggested in the recipes is caster sugar – never use icing sugar as it contains an anti-caking agent.

Stock syrup is the backbone of a sorbet – it is much easier to adjust the sweetness of a sorbet if you combine your fruit or vegetable with pre-prepared stock syrup. This stock syrup undergoes a partial 'inversion' by the addition of fresh lemon juice or cream of tartar (see sucrose inversion, Q & A, page 246). The process of inversion helps prevent crystallisation of the syrup: the newly disengaged fructose and glucose molecules interfere with the remaining sucrose molecules as they try to lock back together again as the syrup is cooling. If you wish to make stock syrup without the fresh lemon juice, follow the same method but simply bring it to the boil and then omit the simmering part, since it is the simmering of the liquid that assists the inversion.

Stock syrup keeps for approximately 1 month if stored in the fridge, but it must be kept in a sealed container in order to avoid any contamination.

MAKES ABOUT 800 g

500 g caster sugar

juice of 1 lemon or 1 tsp cream of tartar (optional)

1 Dissolve the sugar in 500 ml of water by slowly bringing it to the boil, then add the lemon juice or cream of tartar, if using. Turn down the heat and allow it to simmer for 5 minutes until it becomes slightly viscous.

2 Strain, cool and store in a sealed container in the fridge for up to 1 month.

Classics

Here I have chosen a selection of ices that I consider to be some of the 'classics'. By that I do not simply mean the flavours of ice cream that are the most popular, rather those with which I think you will be most familiar. While these flavours may not have the excitement or novelty of the flavour combinations you will find in the chapters that follow, in my opinion there is still little to rival the simple joy that comes from a creamy vanilla ice cream, bursting with flavour from a heady, aromatic vanilla pod, or the bracing sharpness of a lemon sorbet.

vanilla ice cream

SERVES 9–10 (approx. 1.4 kg)

3 vanilla pods
750 ml whole milk
450 ml whipping cream
12 egg yolks
240 g caster sugar
  or 210 g caster sugar and 2 tbsp glucose syrup

1 Halve the vanilla pods and scrape out and retain the seeds.

2 Put the milk and cream in a pan, add the vanilla pods and the seeds, and heat to just below boiling point. Add the glucose syrup, if using, to the milk and cream, and stir until it dissolves. Take off the heat and set aside.

3 Beat the egg yolks with the sugar. Add the warm milk to the egg-sugar mix and return the custard to the pan. Heat the custard, stirring continuously, to 80°C on a probe thermometer and maintain for 15 seconds. Do not allow the mix to boil or it will scramble.

4 Turn off the heat and continue whisking the custard for a few minutes to reduce the heat. Transfer the mix to a container, and place in an ice bath, in order to cool the custard as quickly as possible to 4°C. Once cooled, cover the container and transfer to the fridge to mature for a minimum of 4 hours (or ideally overnight).

5 Remove the vanilla pods from the custard before churning. (The pods can be washed in warm water, dried and put into a jar of sugar in order to make vanilla sugar.) Churn in an ice-cream machine until firm or follow the still-freezing method (see page 43). Put in a sealed container and cover the top of the ice cream with waxed or greaseproof paper. Transfer to the freezer until needed.

very creamy vanilla ice cream

I have included a second vanilla ice cream recipe here because the texture and flavour of this one is quite different from the first. It has a high fat content due to the use of double cream, which gives it a deliciously fresh, rich cream taste, though the vanilla flavours are less immediately discernible because the taste receptors in the tongue and palate are somewhat 'muted' by the fat content. This would be a lovely accompaniment to a fruit tart such as Tarte Tatin.

SERVES 10–11 (approx. 1.6 kg)

3 vanilla pods
500 ml whole milk
900 ml double cream
9 egg yolks
180 g caster sugar
  or 150 g caster sugar and 2 tbsp glucose syrup
a squeeze of fresh orange juice (optional)

Follow the method for Vanilla Ice Cream (page 53), adding the optional orange juice as the custard is cooling.

rum and raisin ice cream

SERVES 7–8 (approx. 1.1 kg)

200 g raisins
200 ml dark rum
500 ml whole milk
250 ml whipping cream
6 egg yolks
150 g soft brown sugar

1 The day before you intend to make the ice cream, put the raisins and the rum into a pan and heat gently for a few minutes without allowing them to boil. Take off the heat and allow to cool. Cover and set aside to soak overnight, allowing the raisins to plump up and absorb most of the liquid.

2 On the following day, put the milk and cream in a pan and heat to just below boiling point. Beat the egg yolks with the sugar. Add the warm milk to the egg–sugar mix and return the mixture to the pan. Heat the custard, stirring continuously, to 80°C on a probe thermometer and maintain for 15 seconds. Do not allow the mix to boil or it will scramble.

3 Turn off the heat and continue whisking the custard for a few minutes to reduce the heat, then transfer the mix to a container, and place in an ice bath, in order to cool the custard as quickly as possible to 4°C.

4 Drain the macerated raisins and set aside. Add the rum to the custard and transfer it to a covered container in the fridge to mature for a minimum of 4 hours (or ideally overnight).

5 Churn in an ice-cream machine until firm or follow the still-freezing method (see page 43). Stir the raisins into the churned ice cream. Put in a sealed container and cover the top of the ice cream with waxed or greaseproof paper. Transfer to the freezer until needed.

dark chocolate ice cream

SERVES 9–10 (approx. 1.4 kg)

500 ml whole milk
500 ml whipping cream
40 g cocoa powder, approx. 4 tbsp
250 g plain chocolate (min. cocoa solids 70 per cent)
3–4 fresh coffee beans (optional)
6 egg yolks
150 g caster sugar

1 Heat the milk and cream in a pan to just below boiling point then take off the heat. Make a paste of the cocoa powder by mixing it with a little of the heated milk and cream. Add the paste to the warm milk-cream and whisk continuously over a very low heat for 4-5 minutes in order to cook out the powdery taste of the cocoa.

2 Break up the chocolate into small pieces and put in a bowl set over a pan of simmering water, stirring from time to time until the chocolate melts. Add the melted chocolate and coffee beans, if using, to the milk and cream, and stir until everything is combined.

3 Beat the egg yolks with the sugar. Add the warm milk to the egg-sugar mix and return the mixture to the pan. Heat the custard, stirring continuously, to 80°C on a probe thermometer and maintain for 15 seconds. Do not allow the mix to boil or it will scramble.

4 Turn off the heat and continue whisking the mix for a few minutes to reduce the heat. Transfer the mix to a container, and place in an ice bath, in order to cool the custard as quickly as possible to 4°C. Once cooled, cover the container and transfer to the fridge to mature for a minimum of 4 hours (or ideally overnight).

5 Strain the custard and discard any coffee beans. Churn in an ice-cream machine until firm or follow the still-freezing method (see page 43). Put in a sealed container and cover the top of the ice cream with waxed or greaseproof paper. Transfer to the freezer until needed.

coffee ice cream

SERVES 4–5 (approx. 700 g)

500 ml whole milk
150 ml whipping cream
40 g ground espresso coffee beans
3 egg yolks
135 g caster sugar
  or 110 g caster sugar and 1 tbsp glucose syrup

1 Combine the milk, cream, ground espresso and glucose syrup, if using, in a pan, and heat to just below boiling point. Remove from the heat and let it infuse for 15 minutes.

2 Strain the milk through a piece of muslin or a coffee filter and pour the milk into a clean pan.

3 Beat the egg yolks with the sugar. Add the warm milk to the egg–sugar mix and return the mixture to the pan. Heat the custard, stirring continuously, until the temperature reaches 80°C on a probe thermometer, ensuring it stays at 80°C for 15 seconds. Do not allow the mix to boil or it will scramble.

4 Turn off the heat and continue whisking the custard for a few minutes to reduce the heat, then transfer the mix to a container, and place in an ice bath, in order to cool the custard as quickly as possible to 4°C. Once cooled, cover the container and transfer to a fridge to mature for a minimum of 4 hours (or ideally overnight).

5 Churn in an ice-cream machine until firm or follow the still-freezing method (see page 43). Put in a sealed container and cover the top of the ice cream with waxed or greaseproof paper. Transfer to the freezer until needed.

lemon sorbet

I like to serve this retro style by removing the pith from the required number of lemons, then freezing the skins and scooping the sorbet into them.

SERVES 6–7 (approx. 1 kg)

500 ml fresh lemon juice (approx. 10–12 lemons,
   of which 2 are unwaxed)
300 g caster sugar
   or 255 g caster sugar and 3 tbsp glucose syrup

1 Wash and dry the two unwaxed lemons then pare the rind into a pan together with the caster sugar and 300 ml of water. Bring to the boil, then reduce the heat and add the glucose syrup, if using. Allow the lemon stock syrup to simmer for 5 minutes until slightly viscous. Strain, discard the rind and allow to cool.

2 Squeeze all the lemons and put the juice through a sieve to remove any sediment and pips. Combine the lemon juice with the lemon stock syrup and churn in an ice-cream machine until firm or follow the still-freezing method (see page 43).

3 Put in a sealed container and cover the top of the sorbet with waxed or greaseproof paper. Transfer to the freezer until needed.

Speedy ices

When you want to make an ice cream quickly but don't want to be bothered with making a custard, you can simply combine a flavour or ingredient with milk and/or cream and sugar and churn the mix in an ice-cream machine or by the 'still-freezing' method. This style of ice-cream making is called the Philadelphia style, or what I call 'speedy ices'. You may find your ice creams are slightly grainier than custard-based ices due to the lack of egg yolks to emulsify the mix, but don't let that prevent you from giving them a go – they really are very speedy and packed full of delicious flavours that can be whipped up in a hurry. ———

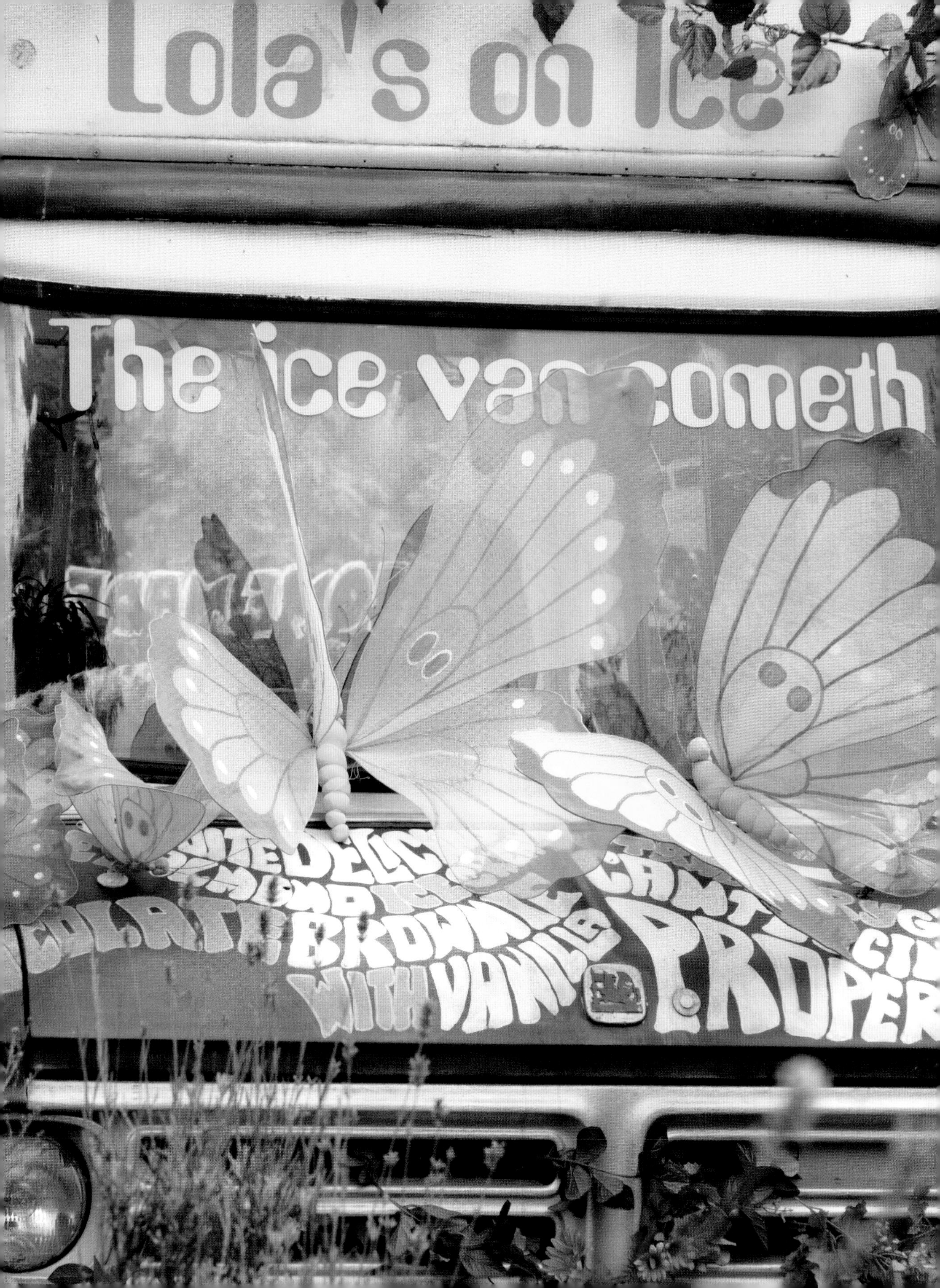
Lola's on Ice

redcurrant ice cream

These delicate, vibrant berries hang like jewels on their stem. When combined with a simple mix of cream and sugar, they make a deliciously flavour intense, slightly tart ice cream. Redcurrants have a high pectin content, which gives the ice cream its firm structure.

SERVES 5–6 (approx. 800 g)

1.05 kg redcurrants
200 ml whipping cream
200 g caster sugar
a squeeze of fresh orange juice

1 Wash the redcurrants. Leaving to one side a few sprigs to use for decoration, remove the stems of the remaining redcurrants and mash them with a fork. Add the cream and sugar.

2 Strain the purée and add the orange juice.

3 Churn in an ice-cream machine until firm or follow the still-freezing method (see page 43). Put in a sealed container and cover the top of the sorbet with waxed or greaseproof paper. Transfer to the freezer until needed.

TO SERVE *Garnish the ice cream with the reserved sprigs of redcurrants. For a 'frosted berry' effect, brush the berries, sprigs and all, with egg white, then dip them in caster sugar and allow them to dry before serving.*

speedy summer fruit ice cream

There are two red summer fruit ice creams in this book, one is a custard based ice cream (see recipe page 103) and the other is this, a speedier version. I like to add raspberries to what is essentially a strawberry ice cream because they bring extra depth of flavour. You could of course, omit the raspberries if you prefer.

SERVES 8 (approx. 1.2 kg)

900 g strawberries
200 g raspberries
200 ml double cream
150 g caster sugar

1 Rinse the berries and drain. Hull the strawberries.

2 Purée all of the ingredients in a blender, then strain a couple of times. Churn in an ice-cream machine until firm or follow the still-freezing method (see page 43).

3 Transfer to a sealed container, covering the top of the ice cream with waxed or greaseproof paper. Transfer to the freezer until needed.

fresh mint ice cream
with chocolate brownies

A French pastry chef brought this ice-cream recipe to Lola's, where it was a firm favourite with our customers for many years. Because it is eggless, it does not have as smooth a texture as an ice cream that has been emulsified. Disregard its textural shortcomings and enjoy an ice cream that is brimming with fresh mint flavours. I serve this from my ice-cream van with chocolate brownies, as a play on 'mint chocolate chip' – it is always extremely popular!

For the brownies, I have used the excellent recipe given to me by Juliet Peston, Lola's first head chef. The brownies are deeply gooey and thoroughly scrumptious and even better the day after they are made, so bake them in advance if you can. The trick is not to let the brownies overcook – keep an eye on the timing and check that your oven is at the correct temperature by using a stand-alone oven thermometer.

SERVES 10–11 (approx. 1.1 kg)

for the ice cream
100 g fresh mint leaves, including stalks
500 ml whole milk
500 ml double cream
130 g caster sugar
  or 100 g caster sugar and 2 tbsp glucose syrup
50 ml crème de menthe (optional)

for the chocolate brownies
240 g plain chocolate
240 g unsalted butter, plus a little extra for buttering
200 g caster sugar
2 medium eggs and 1 medium egg yolk
2 tsp vanilla extract
120 g plain flour, sifted
4 tbsp cocoa powder
1/2 tsp baking powder

1 Wash and dry the mint, and discard any damaged leaves.

2 Heat the milk, cream, sugar, glucose syrup (if using), and mint (including the stalks) to just below boiling point. Remove from the heat and cool.

3 Strain and discard the mint leaves. Add the crème de menthe, if using. Put in a covered container in the fridge for a couple of hours to allow the flavours to develop.

4 Churn in an ice-cream machine till firm. Put in a sealed container and cover the top of the ice cream with waxed or greaseproof paper. Transfer to the freezer until needed.

5 To make the chocolate brownies, pre-heat the oven to 180°C. Meanwhile, chop the chocolate and melt in a bowl set over a pan of simmering water.

6 Cream the butter and sugar. Add the eggs (don't worry if the mixture curdles at this stage) then the vanilla extract and the melted chocolate. Sift the flour, cocoa powder and baking powder into the mix and fold in gently.

7 Butter a 16 x 21 cm shallow baking tray and pour in the brownie mix. Bake in the pre-heated oven for 35 minutes. Cool on a wire tray before cutting into 12 squares.

white chocolate, cardamom and chilli ice cream

I love white chocolate (which strictly speaking is not chocolate at all, as it is made from cocoa butter not the cocoa bean) and it is a great accompaniment to other flavours – mix it with cardamom and chilli and it has a delicious fiery, aromatic flavour, all within the creamy context of an ice cream.

SERVES 7–8 (approx. 1.1 kg)

1 bird's-eye chilli
200 g white chocolate
6 green cardamom pods
500 ml whole milk
100 ml whipping cream
50 g caster sugar

1 Chop up the chocolate into small pieces and set aside.

2 Wash and dry the chilli, then finely dice. Crush the cardamom pods with a pestle and mortar. Heat the milk, cream, sugar, chilli and cardamom seeds and pods to just below boiling point. Take off the heat, add the chocolate and stir until everything is incorporated. Allow to cool.

3 Strain the mix and discard the cardamom and chilli. Churn in an ice-cream machine until firm or follow the still-freezing method (see page 43). Put in a sealed container and cover the top of the ice cream with waxed or greaseproof paper. Transfer to the freezer until needed

plum and earl grey tea ice cream

Plums are rich in antioxidants and a good source of potassium and vitamins C and A, and since this simply prepared ice cream does not have that much cream or sugar in it, it is rather a nice way of persuading one's family to eat nutritious fruit. Adding a bergamot-infused tea bag brings extra smoky aromas to the ice cream.

SERVES 4 (approx. 600 g)

6–7 plums or greengages (approx. 600 g)
100 g caster sugar
1 vanilla pod
1 Earl Grey tea bag
75 ml whipping cream
75 g Greek yoghurt

1 Wash the plums, cut in half and put them, skin-side up, in a wide, shallow pan along with 150 ml of water, sugar and vanilla pod. Heat to just below boiling point, then reduce the heat, add the Earl Grey tea bag and poach the plums, turning them once, for 15–20 minutes or until they are soft. Remove and discard the tea bag. Allow to cool.

2 Remove the stones from the plums and discard the vanilla pod (or reserve for some other use). Put the plums and their syrup into a blender and purée, then add the cream and the yoghurt. Strain, then churn in an ice-cream machine till firm.

3 Put the ice cream in a sealed container and cover the top with waxed or greaseproof paper. Transfer to the freezer until needed.

peanut butter ice cream with salted peanut brittle

Speedy ices are an excellent way of introducing children to the fun of making ice creams. My niece Daisy and nephew Johnny are now experts at making this ice cream, such is its popularity with them and their friends.

SERVES 6–7 (approx. 1 kg)

for the ice cream
400 ml whole milk
400 ml whipping cream
200 g caster sugar
2 tsp vanilla extract
200 g smooth or crunchy peanut butter

for the salted peanut brittle
150 g caster sugar
20 g unsalted butter
200 g roasted salted peanuts

1 To make the ice cream, put the milk, cream and sugar in a pan and bring to just below boiling point. Add the vanilla extract.

2 Put the peanut butter in a mixing bowl and add a couple of tablespoons of the heated-milk mix to the peanut butter, stirring constantly to combine. Gradually add the rest of the heated milk and stir everything together. Allow to cool.

3 Churn the mixture in an ice-cream machine until it is firm or follow the still-freezing method (see page 43). Put in a sealed container and cover the top of the ice cream with waxed or greaseproof paper. Transfer to the freezer until needed.

4 To make the salted peanut brittle, put half of the sugar in a pan over a moderate heat. Stir until the sugar dissolves; it will become crumbly to begin with, but don't worry. Make sure all the sugar is dissolved before you add the remaining sugar. Scrape the bottom and the sides of the pan as you go along until you have added all the sugar. Cook the caramel until it reaches a lovely golden brown.

5 Add the butter and the peanuts and stir them around for a few minutes until the peanuts are coated in the caramel. Pour the mix onto a sheet of foil or non-stick baking paper and allow to cool.

6 Once cooled and hardened, break up the brittle into small or large chunks. If not using immediately, transfer to a container and store in a cool, dry place.

TO SERVE *Scoop the ice cream into bowls and top with the salted peanut brittle.*

dark chocolate, apricot and stem ginger ice cream

SERVES 6–7 (approx. 700 g)

240 g apricots
50 g caster sugar
1 stem ginger, chopped
1 tbsp stem ginger syrup
200 g plain chocolate (min. cocoa solids 70 per cent)
200 g crème fraîche

1 Wash, halve and stone the apricots and put them, skin-side down, in a shallow pan with 150 ml of water, the sugar, stem ginger and stem ginger syrup. Bring to the boil then reduce the heat and simmer for approximately 5 minutes till the apricots are soft. Cool a little, then put everything in a blender and blend to a purée, then strain.

2 Chop the chocolate and put it in a bowl set over a pan of simmering water to melt, stirring occasionally. Stir in the apricot purée followed by the crème fraîche.

3 Churn in an ice-cream machine until firm or follow the still-freezing method (see page 43). Put in a sealed container and cover the top of the ice cream with waxed or greaseproof paper. Transfer to the freezer until needed.

dark chocolate, soya milk, fresh ginger and lemon grass ice cream

A perfect ice cream for vegans or those unable to eat dairy products. It is brimming with the simply gorgeous combination of ginger-and-lemon-grass-flavoured chocolate.

SERVES 4–5 (approx. 700 g)

200 g plain chocolate (min. cocoa solids 70 per cent)
4 lemon grass stalks
20 g fresh root ginger
600 ml soya milk
100 g caster sugar
1 tbsp glucose syrup (optional)
1 lime

1 Chop the chocolate and put it in a bowl. Set aside.

2 Remove the ends and the tough outer leaves of the lemon grass, bruise them with a pestle or rolling pin then roughly chop. Remove the skin from the ginger with a paring knife and chop finely.

3 Put the lemon grass in a pan with the ginger, soya milk, sugar and glucose syrup, if using, and heat the mix to just below boiling point. Pour the hot soya milk over the chocolate and stir with a balloon whisk until the chocolate dissolves. Leave to cool.

4 Strain the chocolate–soya milk mix and discard the lemon grass and ginger. Add the juice of one lime to taste. Churn the mix in an ice-cream machine until it is firm or follow the still-freezing method (see page 43). Put in a sealed container and cover the top of the ice cream with waxed or greaseproof paper. Transfer to the freezer until needed.

Fruit

When fruit is abundant and in season, this is the time to make the most of the harvest and either gobble it up as it is, or convert it into flavour-packed and thoroughly irresistible ice creams, sorbets and granitas. The following recipes are just a small selection of possibilities but it is really worth playing around with different fruits, creating your own recipes to impress family and friends.

apple and cinnamon sorbet

SERVES 3–4 (approx. 500 g)

2 large cooking apples (approx. 700 g)
150 g caster sugar
1 tbsp glucose syrup (optional)
1 cinnamon stick

1 Peel, quarter and core the apples, and put in a pan with 250 ml of water, the sugar, glucose syrup, if using, and cinnamon stick. Bring to the boil, then simmer and cook the apples until tender (about 10 minutes). Cool and discard the cinnamon stick.

2 Blend to a purée then churn in an ice-cream machine until firm or follow the still-freezing method (see page 43). Put in a sealed container and cover the top of the sorbet with waxed or greaseproof paper. Transfer to the freezer until needed.

gooseberry sorbet

SERVES 4 (approx. 700 g)

450 g gooseberries
125 g caster sugar
1 tbsp glucose syrup (optional)

1 Wash the gooseberries then top and tail them using a pair of scissors. Heat 125 ml of water and the sugar in a wide pan and add the glucose syrup, if using, stirring until it all dissolves. Add the gooseberries and cook for approximately 5 minutes, then cool.

2 Put the gooseberry mix into a blender and purée. Strain and discard the pips. Churn in an ice-cream machine until firm or follow the still-freezing method (see page 43). Put in a sealed container and cover the top of the sorbet with waxed or greaseproof paper. Transfer to the freezer until needed.

damson ice cream

By late August, the damson tree overshadowing the garden shed is heavy with dark purple fruit. These delicious relatives of the wild plum are very sharp and can't really be eaten on their own but they are perfect for making into jam or chutney, and, of course, for folding into ice cream.

SERVES 6–7 (approx. 950 g)

450 g damsons
240 g caster sugar
500 ml whole milk
100 ml whipping cream
3 egg yolks

1 Wash the damsons, watching out for and replacing any damaged fruit, and put in a pan with 100 ml of water and half the sugar. Bring to the boil, then reduce the heat and simmer for approximately 5 minutes. Allow to cool.

2 Strain and discard the damson stones. Put in a covered container in the fridge.

3 Heat the milk and cream in a pan to just below boiling point. Beat the egg yolks with the remaining sugar. Add the warm milk to the egg-sugar mix and return the mixture to the pan. Heat, stirring continuously, until the temperature reaches 80°C on a probe thermometer, ensuring it stays there for 15 seconds. Do not allow the mixture to boil or it will scramble.

4 Take off the heat and continue whisking the mix for a few minutes to reduce the heat. Transfer the mix to a container, and place in an ice bath, in order to cool the custard as quickly as possible to 4˚C. Once cooled, fold in the damson purée, cover the container and transfer to the fridge to mature for a minimum of 4 hours (or ideally overnight).

5 Churn in an ice-cream machine until firm or follow the still-freezing method (see page 43). Put in a sealed container and cover the top of the ice cream with waxed or greaseproof paper. Transfer to the freezer until needed.

seville orange marmalade
ice cream

Seville oranges appear for a very brief period in January, and it is an eagerly awaited moment for marmalade makers, who love the tart acidity of this rough- skinned bitter orange.

You can find some excellent Seville orange marmalade in the shops, but I have included a recipe for making the marmalade here because I simply love the intensely fragrant orange aromas that it produces. This is an adaptation from Delia Smith's recipe for Seville Orange Marmalade. You will be making enough marmalade for several batches of ice cream.

SERVES 6–7 (approx 1 kg)

for the marmalade
950 g Seville oranges
1.2 kg caster sugar
1 lemon
knob of butter

for the ice cream
600 g Seville Orange Marmalade
400 g Vanilla Ice Cream (recipe page 53 – omitting the vanilla pod)

1 Wash and dry the oranges then cut them in half and squeeze the juice out of them. Set the juice aside, retaining pips and pith, which will be used for their pectin. Cut the orange halves into quarters and then into thin shreds (there is no need to remove the pith as this will be dissolved once the marmalade boils). Put 2.25 litres of water into a heavy-bottomed pan along with the orange juice, the juice of a lemon and the orange shreds. Cut a square of muslin (approximately 18 cm x 18 cm), put the pips into it, tie it up and place it in the water. Bring the mix up to simmering point and simmer, uncovered, for approximately 2 hours or until the peel is completely softened.

2 Place a couple of saucers to chill in the fridge. Remove the bag of pips from the pan. Add the sugar to the saucepan and stir it over a low heat until it dissolves. Squeeze the bag of pips over the liquid to extract as much pectin as possible. Increase the heat until the mix comes to a boil. After 15 minutes, spoon some of the mixture onto one of the saucers in the fridge and place it back in the fridge. After a few minutes, check the sample marmalade by pushing it with your finger – if it has set it will have a crinkly skin. If it has not, continue boiling the marmalade and repeat the test every 10 minutes or so until you reach setting point. Be careful at this point not to let the marmalade burn as a burnt marmalade flavour is not what you want to achieve!

3 Turn the heat off and leave the marmalade to settle for approximately 20 minutes. Spoon off any scum and add a knob of butter to the mix to disperse the rest.

4 Sterilise some jars either by putting them through a dish-washing cycle, or by washing and drying then heating them in an oven for 5 minutes at 100°C. Spoon the marmalade into the jars then cover with waxed discs or baking parchment while the marmalade is still warm. Store in a cool, dark place until needed.

5 Stir the marmalade into the ice cream and serve.

blood orange granita

Blood oranges come in different varieties, but all of them are smaller than table oranges and have a sweet, slightly bitter and less acidic flavour than other types of orange. The dark pigment in the flesh is due to the presence of anthocyanins, a group of pigments common to many fruit but generally not citrus fruit. Blood orange juice frozen into amber-red crystals looks gorgeous in a bowl and makes a rather seductive supper party dessert.

SERVES 5 (approx. 800 g)

750 ml blood orange juice (approx. 11–12 blood oranges)
100 g caster sugar

1 Juice the oranges and combine the juice with the sugar in a pan and heat till the sugar has dissolved. Allow to cool.

2 Transfer to a covered container in the freezer. After about 1 hour, when the mixture starts to form crystals, stir it with a fork. Ensure that you scrape down the sides and that everything is combined. Replace the container in the freezer.

3 Repeat this procedure every half hour or so until the mixture resembles crushed ice – this may take up to 3 hours.

TO SERVE *Allow the granita to soften a little then scrape the crystals with a spoon into glass bowls or martini glasses.*

mango and passion fruit sorbet

If you have an Asian store near by, pop in and purchase some succulent, Alphonso mangoes. They really are the juiciest of the mango varieties. Of course, you can use any type of mango for this recipe, just make sure they are ripe.

SERVES 5 (approx. 800 g)

1 tbsp glucose syrup (optional)
200 g stock syrup, cooled
2–3 ripe mangoes (approx. 500–600 g mango pulp)
6–7 wrinkly passion fruit (approx. 110 g seedless pulp)

1 Heat the glucose syrup, if using, in a pan with the stock syrup till it dissolves. Set aside to cool.

2 Peel the mangoes, ensuring that you remove as much of the yellow skin (or, in the case of other varieties, green skin) from the flesh as possible. Remove the stone. Cut the flesh into smallish pieces, and put into a blender with the stock syrup. Blend till smooth, then strain.

3 Cut the passion fruit in half, and scoop out the pulp and seeds with a teaspoon. Put them into a strainer set over a bowl and extract as much of the pulp and juice as possible by rubbing them through the strainer with a rubber spatula. Reserve two tablespoons of the seeds and discard the rest.

4 Mix the strained passion fruit with the mango. If you have time, put the fruit mix into a covered container in the fridge for a couple of hours, to allow the flavours to mature.

5 Churn in an ice-cream machine until firm or follow the still-freezing method (see page 43). Put in a sealed container and cover the top of the sorbet with waxed or greaseproof paper. Transfer to the freezer until needed.

TO SERVE *Allow the sorbet to soften a little then scoop into bowls and scatter with the reserved seeds.*

burnt orange caramel ice cream

I have adapted this from another recipe given to me by Juliet Peston. Allowing the caramel partially to 'burn' gives this ice cream a delicious flavour of bitter oranges.

SERVES 9–10 (approx. 1.4 kg)

for the ice cream
500 ml whole milk
6 egg yolks
50 g caster sugar

for the sauce
500 ml fresh orange juice (approx. 5–6 oranges)
250 g caster sugar
50 ml Cointreau (optional)
250 ml whipping cream

1 First make the sauce. Slice the oranges in half, squeeze out the juice and strain to remove the pips. Set aside.

2 Put about a quarter of the 250 g of sugar in a pan set over a moderate heat. Stir until the sugar melts; it will become crumbly to begin with. Make sure all the sugar has melted before you add the next quarter of sugar. Scrape the bottom and the sides of the pan as you go along, and then add the remaining sugar. Once just beyond a medium-dark brown colour, remove the caramel from the heat, or it will continue cooking and the colour will darken even further. It is really a matter of timing to get the caramel to be only marginally 'burnt', not burnt to the point of bitterness; it is best to err on the side of caution, especially when you first make the recipe.

3 Let the caramel stand for a few minutes then stir in the orange juice, little by little, and the Cointreau (if using). The caramel will begin to 'seize up', but just carry on stirring and adding the orange juice until everything is combined. Add the cream and return the pan to a low heat and bring to a gentle boil then reduce the heat further and let it simmer for a few minutes. If you feel the caramel is not dark enough at this point, leave it on the heat for a few more minutes to intensify the flavour. Remove from the heat and set aside to cool.

4 Now make the custard base for the ice cream. Heat the milk in a pan to just below boiling point. Whisk the egg yolks with the 50 g of sugar. Add the warm milk to the egg–sugar mix and return the custard to the pan. Heat, stirring continuously, to 80°C on a probe thermometer and maintain for 15 seconds. Do not allow the mix to boil or it will scramble.

5 Turn off the heat and continue whisking the custard for a few minutes to reduce the heat, then transfer the mix to a container, and place in an ice bath, in order to cool the custard as quickly as possible to 4°C. Add the caramel sauce. Once cooled, cover the container and transfer to the fridge to mature for a minimum of 4 hours (or ideally overnight).

6 Churn in an ice-cream machine until firm or follow the still-freezing method (see page 43). Put in a sealed container and cover the top of the ice cream with waxed or greaseproof paper. Transfer to the freezer until needed.

TO SERVE *This ice cream can be served almost direct from the freezer as the caramel sauce keeps it from becoming too hard.*

rhubarb crumble ice cream

Although I've put this recipe in the Fruit chapter, rhubarb is actually a vegetable and has long been known for its ability to cleanse the blood and purify the system. Forced rhubarb (rhubarb grown in the dark) is available in the winter and is more tender but less flavourful than the rhubarb that appears at the end of March. Rhubarb crumble is, of course, an extremely popular and delicious pudding, and is equally delicious as a crunchy textured ice cream.

SERVES 6 (approx. 900 g)

for the ice cream
500 g whole milk
250 g whipping cream
3 egg yolks
50 g caster sugar

for the crumble
400 g rhubarb
50 g caster sugar
50 g chilled butter
Half a tsp ground ginger
75 g ground almonds
50 g plain flour, sifted

1 Pre-heat the oven to 180°C. Wash the rhubarb, cut into 3 cm lengths and put in a shallow, ovenproof dish. Sprinkle half of the 50 g of sugar over the rhubarb.

2 Dice the chilled butter and rub it into the flour with the tips of your fingers until the mixture resembles fine breadcrumbs. (The butter must be cold or the mixture will become sticky.) Add the ground almonds, the ginger and the remaining sugar. Sprinkle the crumble mix over the rhubarb and bake in the oven for 25–30 minutes, or until the top of the crumble is crispy. Cool, then cover and put in the fridge until needed.

3 To make the custard base for the ice cream: heat the milk and cream to just below boiling point. Whisk the egg yolks with the sugar. Add the warm milk to the egg–sugar mix and return the mixture to the pan. Heat, stirring continuously, to 80°C on a probe thermometer and maintain for 15 seconds. Do not allow the mix to boil or it will scramble.

4 Remove the custard from the heat and continue whisking for a few minutes. Transfer the mix to a container, and place in an ice bath, in order to cool the custard as quickly as possible to 4°C. Once cooled, cover the container and transfer to the fridge to mature for a minimum of 4 hours (or ideally overnight).

5 Churn in an ice-cream machine until firm or follow the still-freezing method (see page 43). Fold the rhubarb crumble into the ice cream then put in a sealed container and cover the top of the ice cream with waxed or greaseproof paper. Transfer to the freezer until needed.

winter fruit ice cream

I have called this recipe a winter fruit ice cream because it includes dried fruits, which I tend to associate with the winter months when fresh fruit is less abundant. Of course, it may be made at any time of the year. This is really a cross between a cassata gelato and zabaglione.

SERVES 7–8 (approx. 1.1 kg)

50 g dried figs
50 g dried apricots, preferably un-sulphured
75 ml Marsala wine
250 ml whole milk
250 ml whipping cream
pinch of ground cinnamon
5 egg yolks
100 g caster sugar

250 g ricotta
50 g pistachios, shelled
50 g candied orange or lemon peel
25 g grated dark chocolate

1 On the day before you want to make your ice cream, remove and discard the stalks from the figs then coarsely chop them along with the apricots, and put the dried fruit in a bowl with the Marsala to macerate overnight.

2 On the following day, heat the milk and cream in a pan to just below boiling point. Add the ground cinnamon.

3 Combine the egg yolks with the sugar. Add the warm milk to the egg-sugar mix and return the mixture to the pan. Heat, stirring continuously, to 80°C on a probe thermometer and maintain for 15 seconds. Do not allow the mix to boil or it will scramble.

4 Remove the custard from the heat and continue whisking for a few minutes to reduce the heat. Transfer the mix to a container, and place in an ice bath, in order to cool the custard as quickly as possible to 4°C. Once cooled, add the ricotta, macerated fruit and Marsala. then cover the container and transfer to the fridge to mature for a minimum of 4 hours (or ideally overnight).

5 Churn in an ice-cream machine or follow the still-freezing method (see page 43) until almost firm. Chop the pistachios and add these to the ice cream mix together with the orange or lemon peel and grated chocolate. Continue churning until firm. Put in a sealed container and cover the top of the ice cream with waxed or greaseproof paper. Transfer to the freezer until needed.

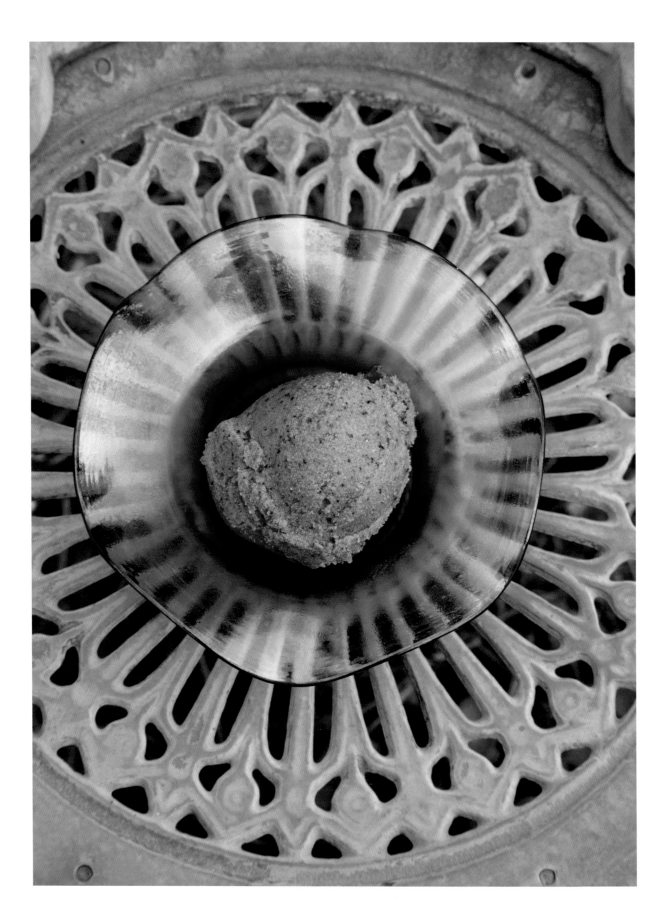

blueberry and banana sorbet

Bananas are rich in potassium and vitamins, while blueberries contain very high levels of antioxidants, which protect the body from the damaging effects of free radicals and the ageing process. So with this recipe up your sleeve there'll be no need for any botox!

SERVES 3–4 (approx. 600 g)

550 g blueberries
150 ml stock syrup, cooled
1 banana
1 tsp fresh lemon juice

1 Wash the blueberries and put them in the blender with the other ingredients. Blend to a purée, then strain.

2 Churn in an ice-cream machine until firm or follow the still-freezing method (see page 43). Put in a sealed container and cover the top of the sorbet with waxed or greaseproof paper. Transfer to the freezer until needed.

lemon curd ice cream

SERVES 4 (approx. 600 g)

5 egg yolks
250 g caster sugar
250 ml fresh lemon juice (approx. 5–6 lemons)
zest of 1 unwaxed lemon
250 ml double cream

1 Beat the egg yolks with the sugar. Add the lemon juice and the lemon zest. Transfer the mixture to a bowl set over a pan of simmering water, ensuring the hot water does not touch the bowl. Whisk constantly until the mixture begins to foam and swell into a soft, frothy mass. If you are using a probe thermometer, heat to 80°C and maintain for 15 seconds.

2 Strain and discard the lemon zest. Transfer the mix to a container that can be placed in an ice bath to cool it. Stir in the whipping cream. Cool the mix as rapidly as possible to 4°C, then put in a covered container in the fridge to mature for a minimum of 4 hours (or ideally overnight).

3 Churn in an ice-cream machine until firm or follow the still-freezing method (see page 43). Put in a sealed container and cover the top of the ice cream with waxed or greaseproof paper. Transfer to the freezer until needed.

banana caramel ice cream with kebabs and toffee sauce

When I go to an event with my ice-cream van, I am always trying to persuade the guests to try new, unusual taste experiences, like Creamy Horseradish or Sweet Miso ice creams (see pages 120 and 187). I always manage to root out adventurous gastrophiles, but, unsurprisingly, it is the old favourites that are the most popular. And one of the most popular is Banana Caramel Ice Cream served with banana 'kebabs' and drizzled in a hot toffee sauce.

In order to get the best out of this ice cream, some advanced planning is required. Buy your bananas about a week in advance, to ensure that they are really ripe by the time you make the ice cream.

SERVES 11–12 (approx. 1.7 kg)

for the ice cream
500 ml whole milk
6 egg yolks
50 g light brown sugar
6 very ripe bananas
a squeeze of fresh lemon juice

for the toffee sauce
500 g caster sugar
100 ml dark rum (optional)
500 ml whipping cream

for the kebabs
1 banana per 3 guests
cocktail sticks

1 First make the toffee sauce. Put about a quarter of the sugar in a pan set over a moderate heat. Stir until the sugar melts; it will become crumbly to begin with. Make sure all the sugar has melted before you add the next quarter of sugar. Scrape the bottom and the sides of the pan as you go along until you have added all the sugar. Cook until it reaches a lovely golden brown.

2 Remove from the heat and let it stand for a few minutes then stir in the dark rum (if using) followed by the cream – it will bubble vigorously and spit, so be careful. Put the pan back on a low heat and bring it to a gentle boil. Give it a good stir so that any 'toffee' bits that may have formed are dissolved. Remove from the heat and set aside.

3 Heat the milk in a pan to just below boiling point. Add half the toffee sauce to the hot milk and stir until it is combined. Transfer the remaining toffee sauce to a covered container in the fridge until the ice cream is ready to be served.

4 Beat the egg yolks with the sugar. Add the warm milk to the egg–sugar mix and return the mixture to the pan. Heat the custard, stirring continuously, to 80°C on a probe thermometer and maintain for 15 seconds. Do not allow the mix to boil or it will scramble. Turn off the heat and continue whisking the custard for a few minutes to reduce the heat. Strain into a container that can be placed on an ice bath to cool the custard as quickly as possible to 4°C.

5 Chop the 6 ripe bananas and immediately put them in a blender with the lemon juice, to prevent discolouration. Purée, adding a little custard, if you like. Fold the banana purée into the custard, then strain. Churn in an ice-cream machine until firm or follow the still-freezing method (see page 43). Put in a sealed container and cover the top of the ice cream with waxed or greaseproof paper. Transfer to the freezer until needed.

TO SERVE *Allow the ice cream to soften so it can be scooped into bowls. Reheat the toffee sauce in a pan and transfer to a serving jug. Cut each of the bananas into about a dozen slices – put 4 slices of banana onto a cocktail stick and insert the banana 'kebab' into the ice cream. Pour the hot toffee sauce over the kebab and ice cream, and serve immediately.*

peach sorbet

SERVES 6 (approx. 900 g)

100 ml stock syrup, cooled
1 tbsp glucose syrup (optional)
900 g ripe peaches
juice of half a lemon

1 If you are using glucose syrup, heat this in a pan together with the stock syrup until it dissolves. Allow to cool.

2 Peel and stone the peaches. Put the peaches in a blender with the cooled stock syrup and blend to a purée. Add the lemon juice. Strain, then churn in an ice-cream machine until firm or follow the still-freezing method (see page 43).

3 Put the sorbet in a sealed container and cover the top of it with waxed or greaseproof paper. Transfer to the freezer until needed.

raspberry sorbet

SERVES 6 (approx. 900 g)

1 tbsp glucose syrup (optional)
200 ml stock syrup, cooled
25 ml kirsch (optional)
800 g fresh raspberries

1 Heat the glucose syrup, if using, in a pan with the stock syrup until it dissolves. Add the kirsch, if using, and allow to cool. (If you are using neither glucose syrup nor kirsch, disregard this step and proceed.)

2 Wash the raspberries and put them in a blender together with the stock syrup. Blend to a purée. Strain to remove the seeds then churn in an ice-cream machine until firm or follow the still-freezing method (see page 43). Put in a sealed container and cover the top of the sorbet with waxed or greaseproof paper. Transfer to the freezer until needed.

TIP *You can also use frozen raspberries, but do not allow them to thaw. Take them from the freezer and put them directly into the blender with the stock syrup. Churning time will be shorter using frozen raspberry purée.*

red summer fruit ice cream

Every summer I take vast quantities of this ice cream to the Big Brother studios, where it is devoured by the presenters, crew and, if there is any left, residents of the Big Brother house. It is fun to watch all the behind-the-scenes activities – not that I really have time, of course; I am far too busy scooping ice cream!

SERVES 12 (approx. 1.8 kg)

100 ml whole milk
250 ml double cream
250 g caster sugar
  or 200 g caster sugar and 3 tbsp glucose syrup
6 egg yolks
1.3 kg strawberries
300 g raspberries

1 Heat the milk and cream in a pan to just below boiling point. If you are using glucose syrup, add this to the milk and cream, and stir until it dissolves. Set aside.

2 Beat the egg yolks with the sugar. Add the warm milk to the egg–sugar mix and return the mixture to the pan. Heat, stirring continuously, to 80°C on a probe thermometer and maintain for 15 seconds. Be particularly careful with this custard – it has a high egg:dairy ratio and is therefore more likely to scramble.

3 Turn off the heat and continue whisking the mix for a few minutes to reduce the heat. Transfer to a container that can be placed in an ice bath to cool the custard as quickly as possible to 4°C.

4 Wash the fruit, then hull the strawberries and purée both fruits in a blender. Strain the purée and fold it into the cooled custard. Transfer the mix to a covered container in the fridge to mature for a minimum of 4 hours (or ideally overnight).

5 Churn in an ice-cream machine until firm or follow the still-freezing method (see page 43). Put in a sealed container and cover the top of the ice cream with waxed or greaseproof paper. Transfer to the freezer until needed.

cherry and almond ice cream

SERVES 6 (approx. 900 g)

500 ml whole milk
100 ml whipping cream
190 g caster sugar
 or 175 g caster sugar and 1 tbsp glucose syrup
200 g ground almonds (if you can buy whole blanched almonds and
 grind them yourself in a coffee grinder, all the better)
3 egg yolks
300 g fresh cherries

1 Heat the milk, cream and glucose syrup (if using) in a pan to just below boiling point. Add the ground almonds, take off the heat and allow the mixture to infuse for 30 minutes, after which strain twice and discard the almonds.

2 Beat the egg yolks with 150 g of sugar, or, if using glucose syrup, with 135 g of sugar. Reheat the strained milk-almond mixture back into a pan and reheat then add this to the egg-sugar mix. Return the mixture to the pan and heat, stirring continuously, until the temperature reaches 80°C on a probe thermometer, ensuring it stays there for 15 seconds. Do not allow to boil or it will scramble.

3 Turn off the heat and continue whisking the mix for a few minutes to reduce the heat. Transfer the mix to a container, and place in an ice bath, in order to cool the custard as quickly as possible to 4˚C. Once cooled, cover the container and transfer to the fridge to mature for a minimum of 4 hours (or ideally overnight) then churn in an ice-cream machine until firm or follow the still-freezing method (see page 43).

4 Wash, stem and pit the cherries, then cut them in half. Put the cherries in a pan with the remaining sugar and 40 ml of water. Bring to the boil then immediately turn off the heat and allow the cherries to cool in the syrup. Strain and fold the cherries into the ice cream. Put in a sealed container and cover the top of the ice cream with waxed or greaseproof paper. Transfer to the freezer until needed.

memphis belle sorbet

The cocktail Memphis Belle seems to come in all sorts of variations, all united by a principal component, Southern Comfort. In my early twenties I lived in New Orleans, working as a waitress in the French Quarter, dishing out Creole gumbos and muffalatas to tourists on Bourbon Street. Of the rainbow of wonderful characters inhabiting the Quarter, there was one person who has captured my imagination to this day. She was an octogenarian in furs and a felt hat who roller-skated around the Quarter followed by a flock of ducks. She would stop off at the place I worked and order a Memphis Belle, before skating off again, maybe in search of another cocktail.

SERVES 4 (approx. 600 g)

500 g puréed apricots (approx. 12 apricots)
100 g caster sugar
4 tbsp Southern Comfort
3 tbsp oloroso sherry
juice of half a lime
fresh or glacé cherries, for serving (optional)

1 Wash, halve and stone the apricots. Put in a pan with 125 ml of water, the sugar, Southern Comfort and sherry. Bring to just below boiling point, then reduce the heat and simmer for approximately 5 minutes until the apricots start to collapse. Cool.

2 Put the apricots, their syrup and the lime juice into a blender, blend to a purée, then strain. If you have time, put the mix in a covered container in the fridge for a couple of hours to allow the flavours to develop.

3 Churn in an ice-cream machine until firm or follow the still-freezing method (see page 43). Put in a sealed container and cover the top of the sorbet with waxed or greaseproof paper. Transfer to the freezer until needed.

TIP *As a cocktail, Memphis Belle is served with a glacé cherry on top, so you could serve the sorbet topped with a glacé cherry or even a fresh one.*

melon and ginger sorbet

SERVES 10–11 (approx 1.1 kg)

200 ml stock syrup
1 stem ginger, chopped
1 tbsp stem ginger syrup
2 Gala melons (approx. 1 kg flesh and juice)

1 Warm the stock syrup in a pan and add the stem ginger and the stem ginger syrup. Leave to infuse for 15 minutes

2 Slice the melons in half and remove the seeds with a tablespoon. Set a sieve over a bowl and put the melon seeds in it so that any juice will drip into the bowl. Press the seeds into the sieve with a tablespoon or spatula to extract as much juice as possible. Discard the seeds. Scoop out the melon flesh with a tablespoon.

3 Combine the juice with the melon flesh and purée in a blender along with the stock syrup and ginger. Strain. If you have time, put the mix in a covered container in the fridge for a couple of hours to allow the flavours to develop.

4 Churn in an ice-cream machine until firm or follow the still-freezing method (see page 43). Put in a sealed container and cover the top of the sorbet with waxed or greaseproof paper. Transfer to the freezer until needed.

TIP *This sorbet develops a metallic flavour after a few days so should be consumed as soon as possible.*

apricot and bay leaf sorbet

Apricots are rich in the antioxidant beta-carotene as well as in iron and potassium, but health benefits aside, who can resist the arrival in May of this soft and succulent fruit with its sweet aromatics and juicy flesh?

The bay leaf is the aromatic leaf of the laurel tree, and it is commonly used in savoury dishes to add depth and flavour due to its distinctive fragrance. Its aromatics work really well with the apricots, giving the sorbet a subtle back note.

SERVES 4–5 (approx. 700 g)

8 fresh apricots
6 bay leaves
1 tbsp glucose syrup (optional)
100 g caster sugar

1 Wash the apricots then halve and stone them. Put the halves, skin-side down, in a pan together with 400 ml of water, the caster sugar, the bay leaves and the glucose syrup (if using). Bring to a gentle boil, reduce the heat and simmer for approximately 5 minutes until the apricots soften. Set aside to cool.

2 Discard the bay leaves. Purée the apricots and their syrup in a blender, then strain. If you have time, cover and put in a fridge for a couple of hours to allow the flavours to develop.

3 Churn in an ice-cream machine until firm. Put in a sealed container and cover the top of the sorbet with waxed paper. Transfer to the freezer until needed.

blackberry granita

When we were children, each September my sister, Lowri-Ann, and I were handed enormous wicker baskets and sent in search of blackberries among the brambly thickets of Glanllynnau farm near Criccieth, where we lived. We would return, many hours later, our bellies full, our baskets thick with glistening berries and our hands and faces stained a rich puce. Our mother would dispatch us to the bath while she roasted a mallard in blackberry sauce or baked a delicious blackberry and apple crumble. Here, I have simply turned the blackberries into beautifully refreshing puce-coloured crystals.

SERVES 5 (approx. 750 g)

500 g blackberries
175 g caster sugar

1 Wash the blackberries and set aside. Heat the sugar and 300 ml of water in a pan to just below boiling point. Take off the heat; add the blackberries and leave to cool.

2 Blend the cooled blackberries to a purée and strain. Transfer to a covered container in the freezer.

3 After about an hour, the mixture will begin to form crystals. Stir the mixture with a fork, ensuring that you scrape down the sides and that everything is combined. Replace the container in the freezer.

4 Remove and repeat this procedure every half hour or so until the mixture resembles crushed ice – this may take up to 3 hours.

TO SERVE *Allow the granita to soften a little then scrape the crystals into glass bowls or martini glasses using a spoon.*

Vegetables

Vegetable-based ice creams can be sweet or savoury, and make brilliant canapés at a party as well as working alone or in combination with another dish – for example, as a topping for a soup, or even as a dessert. Not all vegetables can successfully be made into an ice cream or sorbet, however, as those who tasted my broccoli and spinach ice cream will attest!

I normally add some sugar even to ' savoury' ices because I believe that sugar brings out the primary flavours of an ingredient when it is frozen. Vegetable-based ice creams work best if they have an intrinsic sweetness.

I have put both the yield of a recipe as well as the quantity of canapés that can be made from it. Canapé sizes have been measured at 20 g – this is the equivalent of about a heaped tablespoon of ice cream. I would also serve this amount as an amuse-gueule or as a dollop in a soup. If you wish to serve an ice cream as a stand-alone, divide the yield by 150g per person and serve it in double scoops, as you would for the other recipes in the book.

cucumber raita sorbet

Raita is traditionally served as a cooling accompaniment to a curry, but I think it makes a deliciously refreshing sorbet, and can be served either as a canapé or as a topping in a bowl of soup, especially a spicy one.

SERVES 40 canapés (approx. 800 g)

1 cucumber (approx. 400 g purée)
400 g Greek yoghurt
100 ml stock syrup (cooled)
5 g fresh mint leaves (about 25–30 leaves)

1 Peel and chop the cucumber then place in a blender with the remaining ingredients, and blend to a purée. If you have time, put in a covered container in the fridge for a couple of hours to allow the flavours to develop.

2 Churn in an ice-cream machine till firm. Put in a sealed container and cover the top of the sorbet with waxed or greaseproof paper. Transfer to the freezer until needed.

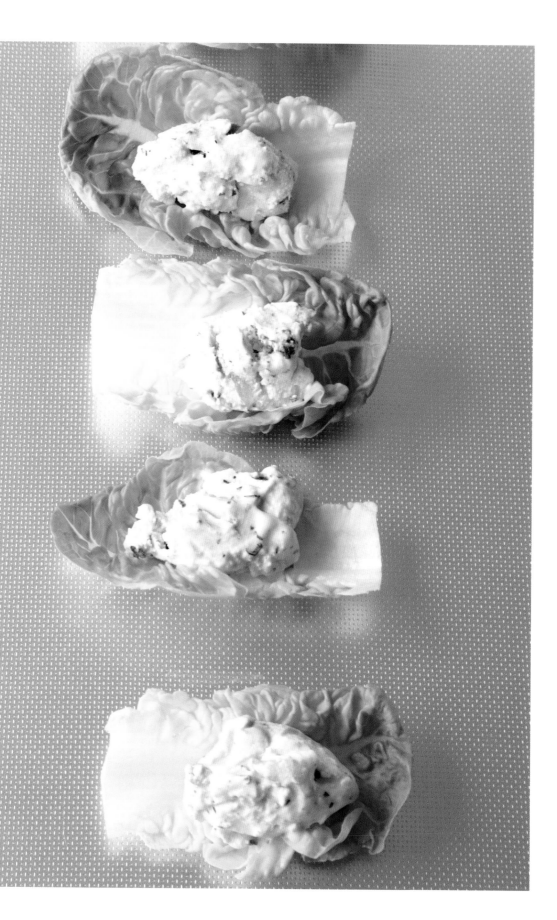

roast red pepper and goats' cheese ice cream

I often bring this ice cream as an extra to events, even if not requested, as it is a favourite of mine and I want as many people as possible to try it. I remember being contacted by the host of a party I attended with my ice-cream van who told me that her twelve-year-old daughter had tasted all of my ice creams and declared this one her absolute favourite. Whenever she went to food shops she would go directly to the vegetable section and hand her mother a couple of glossy red peppers to buy! Now that's my sort of convert!

SERVES 40 canapés (approx. 800 g)

250 g red peppers (about 4 red peppers, after skinning and seeding)
375 ml whole milk
115 g caster sugar
  or 100 g caster sugar and 1 tbsp glucose syrup
100 g goats' cheese
100 g low-fat cream cheese
1 tsp fresh lemon juice

1 Pre-heat the oven to 180°C. Wash the red peppers, put them in an ovenproof dish and roast them in the oven until they collapse (about an hour). Allow to cool.

2 Once the peppers are cool enough to handle, remove and discard the skins and the seeds, as well as any juice. Roughly chop or tear.

3 Heat the milk, sugar and glucose syrup, if using, in a pan to just below boiling point. Cool. Put the milk mix in a blender with the two cheeses and blend. Add the peppers and the lemon juice and blend these too. Strain. Place the mix in a covered container in the fridge for a couple of hours to allow the flavours to develop.

4 Churn in an ice-cream machine until firm or follow the still-freezing method (see page 43). Put in a sealed container and cover the top of the ice cream with waxed or greaseproof paper. Transfer to the freezer until needed.

pea and wasabi sherbet

The idea for this recipe came from munching on wasabi-coated green peas bought in a Japanese food shop. Wasabi is a green horseradish used in Japan as a condiment and known more generally as an accompaniment to sushi. The use of milk in this recipe technically makes it a sherbet, but if you do not wish to include any dairy in the recipe, substitute water for the milk.

SERVES 45 canapés (approx. 950 g)

4 tsp wasabi powder
200 ml whole milk
1 tbsp glucose syrup (optional)
500 g frozen peas
200 ml stock syrup
2 tsp fresh lemon juice

1 Make a paste of the wasabi powder, using a little hot water. Set aside. Heat the milk with the glucose syrup (if using) in a pan to just below boiling point. Add the wasabi paste and stir until thoroughly dissolved. Add the frozen peas, bring back to just below boiling point, then reduce the heat and simmer for 2–3 minutes, stirring occasionally. Allow to cool.

2 Put the mix in a blender and purée. Strain twice. Add the stock syrup and lemon juice. If you have time, put the mix in a covered container in the fridge for a couple of hours for the flavours to develop.

3 Churn in an ice-cream machine until firm or follow the still-freezing method (see page 43). Transfer to a sealed container and cover the top of the sherbet with waxed or greaseproof paper. Transfer to the freezer until needed.

creamy horseradish ice cream

Richard Corrigan, a man who knows a great deal about robust flavours, gave me this recipe on one of his regular visits to Lola's. It is extremely hot so add the horseradish juice little by little, and don't add it all if you feel that your guests won't be able to cope with the fire! If you don't have a juicer, make the recipe omitting the horseradish juice – but it won't be half as hot.

SERVES 40 canapés (approx. 800 g)

1 whole fresh horseradish root
250 ml whole milk
500 ml double cream
3 egg yolks
100 g sugar

1 Peel the horseradish then cut it in half and juice one of the halves. Set aside. The remaining horseradish needs to be infused in the milk and cream – you could grate it (hard work) or simply peel the root.

2 Heat the milk, cream and grated or peeled horseradish, then turn off the heat and allow the horseradish to infuse for 30 minutes. Strain and discard the horseradish.

3 Whisk the egg yolks with the sugar. Add the warm milk to the mix then return to the pan. Heat, stirring continuously, until it reaches 80°C on a probe thermometer. Ensure it stays at 80°C for 15 seconds. Do not allow the mix to boil or it will scramble.

4 Remove the custard from the heat and continue whisking for a few minutes to reduce the heat. Transfer the mix to a container that can be placed in an ice bath to cool it as quickly as possible to 4°C. Once cooled, add the horseradish juice, little by little, until you feel the ice cream will be hot enough . Put the custard in a covered container in the fridge to mature for a minimum of 4 hours (or ideally overnight).

5 Churn in an ice-cream machine until firm or follow the still-freezing method (see page 43). Put in a sealed container and cover the top of the ice cream with waxed or greaseproof paper. Transfer to the freezer until needed.

sweet potato sorbet

SERVES 6–7 (approx. 1 kg)

2 sweet potatoes (approx. 500–600 g)
3 star anise
1 cinnamon stick
250 g Greek yoghurt
350 ml stock syrup (cooled)

1 Pre-heat the oven to 190°C. Halve the sweet potatoes. Crush the star anise and cinammon stick with a pestle and mortar or rolling pin, then sprinkle the spices over the halved sweet potatoes. Wrap each half in foil and roast the potatoes for approximately an hour, or until a knife can be easily inserted into them. Allow to cool.

2 Remove the flesh from the sweet potatoes, discarding the skin and spices. Put the flesh in a blender, along with the remaining ingredients. Blend to a purée. If you have time, transfer the mix to a covered container in the fridge to allow the flavours to develop for a couple of hours.

3 Churn in an ice-cream machine until firm or follow the still-freezing method (see page 43). Put the sorbet in a sealed container, covering the top with waxed or greaseproof paper. Transfer to the freezer until needed.

avocado and orange sorbet

Carla Pinto, the Brazilian food writer, told me that in Brazil avocados are always treated as a dessert. Once, for pudding, Carla made a Creme de Abacate out of an avocado flavoured with orange and lime juice with a little added sugar. It was absolutely delicious, and I couldn't resist adapting the idea into a sorbet. The primary flavour here is of oranges; the avocado really just provides the sorbet with its creamy texture. The Brazilian avocado is about as large as a melon and not easy to find outside of Brazil, so I have adapted the recipe to use any type of avocado you wish, but preferably Hass. Make sure the avocados are very ripe (Carla says almost black). This is lovely either as a canapé or as a dessert, Brazilian style.

SERVES 45 canapes (approx. 950 g)

400 g avocado flesh (approx. 2–3 ripe avocados)
300 ml orange juice, sieved (approx. 5 oranges)
300 ml stock syrup, cooled
juice of 1–2 limes

1 Halve the avocados and scrape out the flesh with a spoon. Put the flesh into a blender with the orange juice and stock syrup. Blend until smooth.

2 Add the juice from the limes, adding a little at a time until you get a citrusy 'bite', without overpowering the primary flavours. If you have time, put the mix in a covered container in the fridge for a couple of hours to allow the flavours to develop.

3 Churn in an ice-cream machine until firm or follow the still-freezing method (see page 43). Put in a sealed container and cover the top of the sorbet with waxed or greaseproof paper. Transfer to the freezer until needed.

beetroot cassis sorbet

I get excited about lots of different flavours of ices and change my mind about which is my favourite on an almost daily basis but Beetroot Cassis Sorbet is definitely one of the ones I come back to most often.

The beetroot and blackcurrant combination is based on a medieval recipe for a jelly. One of the interesting things about it is that it marries the earthiness of beetroot with the sweetness of blackcurrants. Some people taste savoury flavours first, with the sweetness coming on the back palate, and others, the other way round. This may be served as a canapé or as a stand-alone dessert.

SERVES 50 canapés (approx. 1 kg)

600 g beetroot (about 8–9 large beetroots)
250 g blackcurrants or 350 g bottled blackcurrants (without the syrup)
400 ml stock syrup, cooled

1 Pre-heat the oven to 180°C. Roast the beetroot in their skins for 2–3 hours. (If you wish to substitute ready-cooked beetroot, you will need 500 g – make sure, however, that it is packaged in its natural juices without vinegar.)

2 Mash the blackcurrants through a sieve to extract as much pulp and juice as possible. Discard the remaining stalks and skins. Alternatively, put the blackcurrants in a blender and blend to a purée then strain. Combine the stock syrup with the fruit purée, cover and put in the fridge till needed.

3 Once the beetroot is cooked and a knife can easily be inserted into it, remove from the oven and cool.

4 Peel the cooled beetroot and blend the flesh to a purée. Strain. Combine the beetroot purée with the blackcurrant purée. If you have time, put the mix in a covered container in the fridge for a couple of hours to allow the flavours to develop.

5 Churn in an ice-cream machine till firm or follow the still-freezing method (see page 43). Put in a sealed container and cover the top with waxed or greaseproof paper. Transfer to the freezer until needed.

beetroot and tomato ice cream

The idea for this comes from Skye Gyngell's recipe for pheasant with beetroot and tomato purée in her book *A Year in My Kitchen*. I like to turn pretty much everything into an ice cream these days (including my duvet), and I'd have chucked a bit of pheasant into this recipe as well if I didn't think you'd feel that might be one step too far.

SERVES 45 canapés (approx. 950 g)

450 g beetroot (about 6–7 large beetroots)
275 g tomatoes (about 3–4 medium-sized tomatoes)
200 g crème fraîche
275 ml stock syrup, cooled
a pinch of salt, to season

1 Pre-heat the oven to 180°C. Roast the beetroot in their skins for 2–3 hours, then allow to cool. (If you wish to substitute ready-cooked beetroot, you will need a 500 g-packet – make sure, however, that it is packaged in its natural juices without vinegar.)

2 Reduce the oven temperature to 100°C. Halve the tomatoes and put them in an ovenproof dish. Sprinkle a little salt on them and roast for 3–4 hours or until they have shrivelled. In the meantime, remove the skins from the beetroot and chop. Cover and put in the fridge.

3 Once the tomatoes have cooked, cool, then peel and discard the skins. Place the tomatoes in a blender with the beetroot, crème fraîche and stock syrup. Blend to a purée. If you have time, transfer the mix to a covered container in the fridge for a couple of hours to allow the flavours to develop.

4 Churn in an ice-cream machine until firm or follow the still-freezing method (see page 43). Put in a sealed container and cover the top of the ice cream with waxed or greaseproof paper. Transfer to the freezer until needed.

TO SERVE *Cut medium-sized tomatoes in half, scoop out the flesh and seeds, put a scoop of the ice cream into each half and serve with a teaspoon wedged in.*

cucumber granita

SERVES 4–5 (approx. 500 g)

400 g cucumber (approx. 350 g peeled cucumber)
5 g fresh mint leaves (about 20–25 leaves)
100 g stock syrup, cooled

1 Peel and roughly chop the cucumber, put in a blender with the mint and stock syrup, and blend till smooth. Strain, then transfer the mixture to a covered container in the freezer.

2 After about an hour, when the mixture starts to form crystals, stir it with a fork, ensuring that you scrape down the sides and everything is combined. Return the container to the freezer.

3 Remove and repeat this procedure every half hour or so until the mixture resembles crushed ice – this may take up to 3 hours. Serve by scraping the crystals from the frozen granita with a tablespoon into glass bowls or martini glasses.

parsnip and cider ice cream with apple crisps

Though this idea might sound a little strange I happen to think it is absolutely delicious and another great way to get grown-ups to eat their roots, as it were. It was while I was pondering on my various disasters with curried parsnip and apple ice cream that my old university friend John Butler suggested I should forget the curry and the apples, and just play around with cider. Since I recalled him being a pretty deft hand in the kitchen, I gave it a go.

Parsnips have a natural sweetness and of course are continually crying out to be turned into something more interesting than a mere soup or the role of sidekick for the roast on a Sunday. I have followed John's advice and reserved the curry for some other moment of insanity; the apples remain in the form of cider, of course, as well as in the crisps, which make a delicious accompaniment. I serve this as a dessert.

SERVES 6–7 (approx. 1 kg)

for the ice cream
300 g whole milk
300 g crème fraîche
4 egg yolks
150 g caster sugar
3 parsnips, scrubbed (do not peel them as much of the nutrients
   will be lost if you do)
1.3 litres sweet cider
1 cinnamon stick

for the crisps
2 apples
Juice of 1 lemon
50 ml stock syrup, cooled

1 Heat the milk and crème fraîche in a pan to just below boiling point.

2 Beat the egg yolks with the sugar. Add the warm milk to the egg–sugar mix and return the mixture to the pan. Heat, stirring continuously, until the temperature reaches 80°C on a probe thermometer and remains at that temperature for 15 seconds. Do not allow the mix to boil or it will scramble.

3 Turn off the heat and continue whisking for a few minutes to reduce the heat. Transfer to a container, and place in an ice bath, in order to cool the custard as quickly as possible to 4°C.

4 Meanwhile, top and tail the parsnips, remove and discard the inner core and chop them into pieces approximately 5 cm long. Put the pieces in a pan together with the cider and cinnamon stick, bring to the boil then reduce the heat and simmer for 1½ hours or until the parsnips are very, very tender and most of the liquid has been absorbed. (If most of the liquid has disappeared and the parsnips are still not soft, add some water and continue cooking.)

5 Transfer half the parsnips to a blender, add a little of the cooled custard, and blend. Add the remaining parsnips, a little more custard, if necessary, and blend until smooth. Strain the mix two or three times in order to remove any fibrous material.

6 Combine the parsnip mix with the remaining custard. Cover the container and put in the fridge to mature for a minimum of 4 hours (or ideally overnight). Churn in an ice-cream machine until firm or follow the still-freezing method (see page 43). Put in a sealed container and cover the top of the ice cream with waxed or greaseproof paper. Transfer to the freezer until needed.

7 To make the apple crisps, pre-heat the oven to 100°C and line a baking sheet with non-stick baking paper or foil.

8 Wash and dry the apples, then slice them, as thinly as possible, vertically. Squeeze lemon juice onto the slices as you go, in order to avoid discolouration.

9 Dip the apple slices in the stock syrup then place on the prepared baking sheet and bake in the pre-heated oven for a couple of hours until crisp, keeping an eye on them so that they do not overcook. Cool, then place in an airtight container until needed.

'guacamole' sorbet

I was making an avocado sorbet one day for a client who had requested it for his birthday party and decided that I really wasn't satisfied with the end result – which didn't have enough dynamics in the flavours, in spite of generous amount of lime juice. I found that adding some tomatoes and chilli peppers into the mix made it much more punchy against the backdrop of the creamy avocado. It isn't a proper take on guacamole of course because it lacks the coriander, onions and garlic (which I thought was a wise omission!).

SERVES 60 canapés (approx. 1.2 kg)

4 large ripe avocados, Hass are good (approx. 600 g avocado flesh)
6–8 tomatoes (approx. 200 ml tomato juice)
200 ml stock syrup, cooled
juice of 3 limes
a pinch of salt
1/2 tsp finely chopped red chilli pepper

1 Scoop the flesh from the avocados and put into a blender with all the other ingredients and 300 ml of water. Blend until smooth. Strain the mix and, if you have time, cover and put in the fridge for a couple of hours for the flavours to develop.

2 Churn in an ice-cream machine. Put in a sealed container and cover the top of the sorbet with waxed or greaseproof paper. Transfer to the freezer until needed.

Nuts, herbs and spices

One of the many fabulous things about ice cream is that it is a blank canvas on which to experiment: your imagination can run naked and wild around the aisles of a supermarket or forage and sniff among the thrilling produce of a farmers' market. All sorts of nuts – lightly roasted or made into a praline – may be added to an ice cream to give it a delicious crunch. Or you can imagine yourself in a souk and let the heady, enticing aromas of its myriad spices and herbs inspire you to create unusual and compelling ice creams.

honey and lavender ice cream

There is nothing quite like the flavour of fresh lavender combined with the subtle aromatics of honey in a creamy ice cream.

SERVES 6 (approx. 900 g)

500 ml whole milk
250 ml whipping cream
2 fresh lavender sprigs
6 egg yolks
170 g honey

1 Heat the milk, cream and lavender sprigs in a pan to just below boiling point. Turn off the heat and let the lavender infuse in the liquid for 15 minutes. Strain and discard the lavender, then return the mix to the pan.

2 Whisk the egg yolks, add the infused milk, then return the mixture to the pan. Heat, stirring continuously, to 80°C on a probe thermometer and maintain for 15 seconds. Do not allow the mix to boil or it will scramble.

3 Turn off the heat and continue whisking the mix for a few minutes to reduce the heat. Add the honey and stir it in until thoroughly incorporated. Transfer the mix to a container that can be placed on an ice bath to cool the custard to 4 degrees c as quickly as possible.Cover the container and put in the fridge to mature for a minimum of 4 hours or overnight.

4 Churn in an ice-cream machine till firm or follow the still-freezing method (see page 43). Put in a sealed container and cover the top of the ice cream with waxed or greaseproof paper. Transfer to the freezer until needed.

chilli, lime and yoghurt sherbet

This is a really refreshing sorbet to serve on a hot summer's day and so easy to make. It works really well when partnered with the 'Guacamole' Sorbet (see page 131), both of which are zesty and hot, but the yoghurt provides a refreshing foil.

SERVES 32 canapés (approx. 650 g)

3 bird's-eye chillies, seeded and chopped
500 g Greek yoghurt
200 ml stock syrup, cooled
1 lime

1 Mix together the seeded and chopped chillies with all the other ingredients. Leave to infuse for half an hour.

2 Strain the mix to remove the chillies. Churn in an ice-cream machine until firm or follow the still-freezing method (see page 43). Put in a sealed container and cover the top of the sorbet with waxed or greaseproof paper. Transfer to the freezer until needed.

lemon balm and poppy seed ice cream

Lemon balm has subtle aromatic flavours and is an easy herb to grow, but if you cannot find it, use lemon verbena instead.

SERVES 4 (approx. 600 g)

approx. 30 lemon balm leaves
600 ml whole milk
2 tbsp glucose syrup (optional)
3 egg yolks
125 g caster sugar
25 g poppy seeds

1 Wash the lemon balm and place the leaves in a pan with the milk and glucose syrup, if using. Heat to just below boiling point. Infuse for 30 minutes then discard the leaves.

2 Whisk the egg yolks with the sugar. Add the warm milk to the egg mix and return the mixture to the pan. Heat, stirring continuously, to 80°C on a probe thermometer and maintain for 15 seconds. Do not allow the mix to boil or it will scramble.

3 Remove the custard from the heat and continue whisking for a few minutes to reduce the heat. Transfer the mix to a container, and place in an ice bath, in order to cool the custard as quickly as possible to 4°C. Once cooled, cover the container and transfer to the fridge to mature for a minimum of 4 hours (or ideally overnight).

4 Churn in an ice-cream machine until firm or follow the still-freezing method (see page 43). Once firm, stir in the poppy seeds and transfer the ice cream to a sealed container, covering the surface with waxed or greaseproof paper. Transfer to the freezer until needed.

TO SERVE *The ice cream can be sprinkled with more poppy seeds before serving.*

pecan butterscotch ice cream

When I worked at Le Caprice, Mayfair, in the early 1990s, this ice cream used to appear regularly on the menu and was extremely popular with both adults and children. It was a particular favourite of a well-known politician, who would sometimes dine at the restaurant twice in one day – for lunch with his mistress and for dinner with his wife. Pudding was always Pecan Butterscotch Ice Cream, whoever he was with!

Butterscotch sauce is essentially caramel sauce but is traditionally made from brown sugar and cream with the addition of butter. This is an adaptation of the original recipe served at Le Caprice.

SERVES 6–7 (approx. 1 kg)

for the ice cream
250 g light brown sugar
50 g unsalted butter
250 ml whipping cream
250 ml whole milk
250 ml clotted cream
4 egg yolks
50 g caster sugar

for the pecan praline
100 g pecan nuts
150 g caster sugar

1 Put about a quarter of the brown sugar in a pan set over a moderate heat. Stir until the sugar dissolves; it will become crumbly to begin with, but don't worry. Make sure all the sugar is dissolved before you add the next quarter of sugar. Scrape the bottom and the sides of the pan as you go along and then add the remaining sugar. Cook the caramel until it turns a lovely golden brown.

2 Remove from the heat, add the butter then the whipping cream and stir until everything is thoroughly mixed in – the sauce will spit and froth, so be careful.

3 Heat the milk and clotted cream in a pan to just below boiling point, then add approximately half of the butterscotch sauce to the mix, stirring well. Transfer the remaining butterscotch sauce to a container and chill. (This is added to the ice cream along with the pecan praline for a 'ripple' effect just before the ice cream is served.)

4 Whisk the egg yolks with the sugar. Add the warm milk to the egg-sugar mix and return the mixture to the pan. Heat, stirring continuously, to 80°C on a probe thermometer and maintain for 15 seconds. Do not allow the mix to boil or it will scramble.

5 Turn off the heat and continue whisking the mix for a few minutes to remove some heat. Transfer the mix to a container, and place in an ice bath, in order to cool the custard as quickly as possible to 4°C. Once cooled, cover the container and transfer to the fridge to mature for a minimum of 4 hours (or ideally overnight).

6 Churn in an ice-cream machine until firm or follow the still-freezing method (see page 43). Put in a sealed container and cover the top of the ice cream with waxed or greaseproof paper. Transfer to the freezer until needed.

7 For the praline, heat the oven to 175°C. Line a baking sheet with non-stick baking paper and set aside. Roast the pecans in an ovenproof dish for 10 minutes.

8 Put about a quarter of the sugar in a pan set over a moderate heat. Stir until the sugar melts; it will become crumbly to begin with, but don't worry. Make sure all the sugar has melted before you add the next quarter of sugar. Scrape the bottom and the sides of the pan as you go along and then add the remaining sugar. Cook the caramel until it turns a lovely golden brown.

9 Add the roasted pecans to the caramel, stirring them around until the nuts are coated. Pour the praline mix out on to the baking sheet and, once cool, smash with a rolling pin or pestle into rough chunks. Store in an airtight jar until needed.

TO SERVE *Allow the ice cream to soften a little, then stir in the reserved butterscotch sauce to make a 'ripple' effect. Add the pecan praline to the ice cream, keeping back a little to scatter over the top.*

rosemary ice cream

Although rosemary is an evergreen plant and is available all year round, in April its fragrant blue flowers appear; these are highly scented but less fierce than the leaves. In this recipe I have opted to use the leaves as they are more readily available, but if you do have your own rosemary bush, try using the flowers when they first appear (or candy them for sprinkling on top of your ice cream).

SERVES 4 (approx. 600 g)

3–4 fresh rosemary sprigs
500 ml whole milk
100 ml whipping cream
100 g caster sugar
  or 85 g caster sugar and 1 tbsp glucose syrup
3 egg yolks

1 Wash and dry the rosemary and heat to just below boiling point in a pan with the milk, cream and glucose syrup (if using). Turn off the heat and allow the rosemary to infuse for 15 minutes. Strain the milk and discard the rosemary.

2 Whisk the egg yolks with the sugar. Add the warm milk to the egg mix and return the mixture to the pan. Heat, stirring continuously, to 80°C on a probe thermometer and maintain for 15 seconds. Do not allow the mix to boil or it will scramble.

3 Remove the custard from the heat and continue whisking for a few minutes to reduce the heat, then transfer the mix to a container, and place in an ice bath, in order to cool the custard as quickly as possible to 4°C. Once cooled, cover the container and transfer to the fridge to mature for a minimum of 4 hours (or ideally overnight).

4 Churn in an ice-cream machine until firm or follow the still-freezing method (see page 43). Put in a sealed container and cover the top of the ice cream with waxed or greaseproof paper. Transfer to the freezer until needed.

TIP *Don't worry if you feel the rosemary is too strong once you have made the custard – once it is frozen the flavours will be muted.*

lemon verbena and nettle
ice cream with chickweed 'salad'

' Weed rather not!' No, don' t say that. Go on, really, don' t you feel righteous even just thinking about it? You don' t? You' ll have no worries about your carbon footprint, and gardeners will just love you. Well, all right, the chickweed salad is a little affectation, but since chickweed can be used in a salad or boiled as a vegetable, there is no reason why it cannot be turned into a very pretty dessert ' salad' on the plate looking, as it does, like a garland.

Now, as for the nettles, on their own they can be a little bitter, but the aromatics of the lemon verbena mute this, so that you get all the lovely herbaceous flavours of the nettles with the sweet, lemony scent of the verbena. If you can' t find lemon verbena leaves, try lemon balm or even fresh mint; if your garden, or those of your neighbours are chickweed-free, use pea shoots.

Please note you will need to use gloves to handle the nettles.

SERVES 5–6 (approx. 800 g)

for the ice cream
15 large nettle leaves
20 lemon verbena leaves
500 ml whole milk
250 ml whipping cream
150 g caster sugar
   or 135 g caster sugar and 1 tbsp glucose syrup
3 egg yolks

for the salad
a little icing sugar
a pinch of garam masala
a few fresh chickweed sprigs

1 To make the ice cream, wash and dry the nettles and lemon verbena leaves, and heat them in a pan with the milk, cream and glucose syrup, if using, to just below boiling point. Turn off the heat and allow to infuse for 15 minutes. Put everything in a blender and blitz. Strain twice, and discard any fibres in the strainer.

2 Whisk the egg yolks with the sugar. Add the warm milk-cream to the egg-sugar mix a little at a time and return the mixture to the pan. Heat the mix, stirring continuously, to 80°C on a probe thermometer and maintain for 15 seconds. Do not allow the custard to boil or it will scramble.

3 Turn off the heat and continue whisking the mix for a few minutes to reduce the heat. Transfer the mix to a container, and place in an ice bath, in order to cool the custard as quickly as possible to 4°C. Once cooled, cover the container and transfer to the fridge to mature for a minimum of 4 hours (or ideally overnight).

4 Churn in an ice-cream machine until firm or follow the still-freezing method (see page 43). Put in a sealed container and cover the top of the ice cream with waxed or greaseproof paper. Transfer to the freezer until needed.

TO SERVE *Allow the ice cream to soften. Mix the icing sugar in a bowl with the garam masala. Wash and dry the chickweed, and dip the sprigs in the curried icing sugar. Serve two scoops of ice cream in a bowl with the chickweed sprigs alongside.*

pistachio kulfi

Kulfi is a traditional Indian iced dessert, made from boiled milk reduced to a fraction of its volume, which is not churned, just frozen in moulds. Several recipe books suggest making kulfi with whole milk, but I prefer the more traditional method of using evaporated milk and sweetened condensed milk, which produces a cooked-milk, butterscotch flavour. If you have lollipop moulds, use these, otherwise use dariole moulds; if you have neither, defy tradition and just churn your mixture.

SERVES 8

4 cardamom pods
400 ml evaporated milk
400 ml whipping cream
1 tbsp caster sugar
250 g shelled unsalted pistachio nuts
200 ml condensed milk

1 Lightly crush the cardamom pods so they spilt and put them in a pan with the evaporated milk, cream and sugar. Heat to just below boiling point, then turn off the heat and allow the cardamom pods to infuse for 30 minutes.

2 Strain and discard the pods. Put the milk and 200 g of the pistachio nuts into a blender and blend thoroughly. Reserve the remaining pistachios for crushing and scattering over the kulfis when you serve them.

3 Stir in the condensed milk. Allow the mix to cool before distributing it among eight moulds. Cover the tops with foil and put in the freezer. It will take at least 5-6 hours before they are ready.

TO **SERVE** *If you are using dariole moulds, dip these into a bowl of warm water for about 10 seconds to loosen the sides, ensuring the water does not go over the edge. Serve on a plate and scatter crushed pistachios over them.*

saffron and star anise ice cream

If you have ever wanted to create a really yellow ice cream, this is it! Saffron comes from a flowering plant related to the crocus family. Kashmir saffron is the costliest of all spices as it takes 225,000 hand-picked threads to produce half a kilo of it. Fortunately, there is a less expensive saffron to be found called La Mancha saffron, which is not of the same quality but still jolly good.

SERVES 10 (approx. 1.5 kg)

900 ml whole milk
300 ml whipping cream
240 g caster sugar
  or 210 g caster sugar and 2 tbsp glucose syrup
6 star anise
3 pinches of saffron
9 egg yolks
a squeeze of fresh orange juice (optional)

1 Heat the milk, cream, glucose syrup, if using, star anise and saffron in a pan to just below boiling point. Turn off the heat and leave the ingredients to infuse for half an hour. Remove the star anise and discard.

2 Beat the egg yolks with the sugar. Add the warm milk to the egg mix and return the mixture to the pan. Heat, stirring continuously, to 80°C on a probe thermometer and maintain for 15 seconds. Do not allow the mix to boil or it will scramble.

3 Remove the custard from the heat and continue whisking for a few minutes to reduce the heat. Transfer the mix to a container, and place in an ice bath, in order to cool the custard as quickly as possible to 4°C. Once cooled, stir in the orange juice, if using, cover the container and transfer to the fridge to mature for a minimum of 4 hours (or ideally overnight).

4 Churn in an ice-cream machine till firm or follow the still-freezing method (see page 43). Put in a sealed container and cover the top of the ice cream with waxed or greaseproof paper. Transfer to the freezer until needed.

nutmeg ice cream

SERVES 7–8 (approx. 800 g)

375 ml whole milk
225 ml whipping cream
1 tsp grated nutmeg (preferably freshly grated from a whole nutmeg)
120 g caster sugar
   or 105 g caster sugar and 1 tbsp glucose syrup
5 egg yolks

1 Heat the milk, cream, grated nutmeg and glucose syrup, if using, in a pan to just below boiling point. Turn off the heat and infuse for half an hour.

2 Beat the egg yolks with the sugar. Add the warm milk to the egg–sugar mix and return the mixture to the pan. Heat, stirring continuously, to 80°C on a probe thermometer and maintain for 15 seconds. Do not allow the mix to boil or it will scramble.

3 Remove the custard from the heat and continue whisking for a few minutes to remove some heat. Transfer the mix to a container, and place in an ice bath, in order to cool the custard as quickly as possible to 4°C. Once cooled, cover the container and transfer to the fridge to mature for a minimum of 4 hours (or ideally overnight).

4 Churn in an ice-cream machine until firm or follow the still-freezing method (see page 43). Put in a sealed container and cover the top of the ice cream with waxed or greaseproof paper. Transfer to the freezer until needed.

fresh mint granita

This is such a refreshing granita at any time of day – and, of course, a perfect aid to digestion at the end of the meal.

SERVES 4–5 (approx. 700 g)

100 g mint, including stalks
250 ml stock syrup
25 ml vodka (optional)
a squeeze of fresh lemon juice

1 Wash and dry the mint leaves, and put them in a pan with the stock syrup and vodka, if using. Bring to the boil, then remove the pan from the heat and allow the mint to infuse for 15 minutes. Strain, discard the mint and allow to cool.

2 Add 500 ml of water to the mint mix then put in a shallow sealed container in the freezer.

3 When, after about an hour, the mixture starts to form crystals, stir with a fork, ensuring that you scrape down the sides and that everything is combined. Return the container to the freezer.

4 Remove and repeat this procedure every half an hour or so until the mixture resembles crushed ice – this may take up to 3 hours. Serve by scraping the crystals from the frozen granita with a spoon.

Celebration and dinner party

Ooh, I do love a good party, don't you? The recipe for a successful one being very simple: friends and family – as many of them as you can squeeze into your home without breaking any fire regulations or the furniture. The other elements of your party, such as the food and drink, can be as simple or complicated as you like.

The recipes in this chapter are perfect for celebratory or special occasions; although having home-made ice cream makes any occasion feel like a special one to me.

welsh rarebit ice cream with french toast

Once, while pondering on whether to serve the cheese course before dessert at a supper party, or vice versa, I thought I might amuse my guests (and myself) by creating a savoury dessert. Yes, I know it's a bit silly, but there is nothing like engaging your guests with a little light-hearted fun every now and then. They can always skip the ice cream and eat the French toast if they are too grown-up for this sort of thing.

SERVES 8 single scoops (approx. 600 g)

for the ice cream
400 ml whole milk
150 ml whipping cream
175 g caster sugar
100 g mature Cheddar, grated
2 tsp English mustard
1/2 tsp Worcestershire sauce
4 drops Tabasco sauce
100 ml Guinness
75 g low-fat cream cheese

for the French toast
5 eggs
100 g caster sugar
2 drops vanilla extract
100 ml whole milk
10 slices brioche or white bread
20 g unsalted butter
a little icing sugar and 1/2 tsp ground cinnamon, for dusting

1 For the ice cream, heat the milk, cream and sugar to just below boiling point, then add the grated Cheddar and continue cooking for a few minutes on a low heat until the cheese has melted, stirring occasionally. Add the mustard, Worcester sauce, Tabasco and Guinness. Cool.

2 Put the mix into a blender with the cream cheese and blend, then strain a couple of times. If you have time, leave the mix in a covered container in the fridge for a couple of hours to allow the flavours to develop.

3 Churn in an ice-cream machine until firm or follow the still-freezing method (see page 43). Put in a sealed container and cover the top of the ice cream with waxed or greaseproof paper. Transfer to the freezer until needed.

4 For the French toast, whisk the eggs, sugar and vanilla extract together in a bowl. Add the milk. Dip the brioche or white bread slices into the mix, leaving them to soak for a couple of minutes.

5 Heat a wide, shallow pan and add the butter. Pan fry both sides of the brioche or bread until crispy on the outside.

6 Mix some icing sugar with the cinnamon and shake over the French toast.

TO SERVE *Allow the ice cream to soften before serving. Put the French toast on a plate while still hot and top with a single scoop of the ice cream.*

parmesan ice cream

Every June I drive my ice-cream van to Holland Park, London, to attend a party given by Audrey Meissner to celebrate the birthdays of her daughter Lulu and her son Max. On one occasion, I brought Parmesan Ice Cream to the party, and Audrey's chef, Cristina Yumul, suggested that a quenelle of the ice cream placed in a bowl of chilled tomato soup would make a perfect starter at a supper party.

I followed her suggestion, and she was right! Of course, Parmesan Ice Cream is also delicious served as a canapé with Pear Sorbet (see page 199). You could always replace some of the double cream with virgin olive oil and throw in some basil leaves to make a kind of deconstructed pesto ice cream. If you love ices, the possibilities are endless!

SERVES 40 canapés (approx. 800 g)

500 ml whole milk
200 ml double cream
100 g caster sugar
  or 85 g caster sugar and 1 tbsp glucose syrup
250 g freshly grated Parmesan
black pepper, for seasoning

1 Heat the milk, cream, sugar and glucose syrup, if using, in a pan to just below boiling point. Add the Parmesan and black pepper, and stir the mix so that the cheese melts. It will seem a little oily and granular at this point, but don't worry. Allow to cool.

2 Put the cooled mix in a blender and blend till smooth. Strain twice. Transfer to a covered container in the fridge for a couple of hours to allow the flavours to develop.

3 Churn in an ice-cream machine until firm or follow the still-freezing method (see page 43). Put in a sealed container and cover the top of the ice cream with waxed or greaseproof paper. Transfer to the freezer until needed.

crab ice cream with sorrel sherbet

One ice-cream manufacturer based in Japan produces rather challenging flavoured ice creams, including some made from cactus, chicken wings, ox tongue and eel. While I would feel duty bound to taste their whole range, given the opportunity, I feel less inclined to perform my own alchemy of this kind. Crab ice cream, on the other hand (which also appears in their range), was an immediate inspiration, because it is really just a step away from a chilled crab bisque or prawn cocktail, so why should it not make a lovely canapé or starter on a hot summer's day? I have chosen to pair the Crab Ice Cream with Sorrel Sherbet. Sorrel sauce is often served as an accompaniment to fish, and also works well as a foil for the Crab Ice Cream.

I like to serve this combination in shot glasses with the Sorrel Sherbet scooped into the bottom half of the shot glasses topped with the Crab Ice Cream, or as a starter with both ices placed into a crab shell. Your guests will taste the richness of the crab first, followed by clean, refreshing flavours of the Sorrel Sherbet. Alternatively, serve the crab ice cream on its own as a starter, placed on half a very ripe avocado and a wedge of lemon.

SERVES 45 canapés (approx. 900 g)

for the ice cream
500 ml fresh fish stock
200 ml whole milk
200 ml double cream
3 large egg yolks
150 g caster sugar
150 g cooked brown crab meat
100 g cooked white crab meat
2 tsp fresh lemon juice

for the sherbet
90 g sorrel leaves
750 g Greek yoghurt
300 ml stock syrup, cooled

1 For the ice cream, bring the fish stock to the boil then reduce the heat and simmer for 5 minutes. Add the milk and cream.

2 Beat the egg yolks with the sugar. Add the warm milk–fish stock to the egg–sugar mix then return the mixture to the pan. Heat, stirring continuously, to 80°C on a probe thermometer and maintain for 15 seconds. Do not allow the mix to boil or it will scramble.

3 Take off the heat and continue whisking for a few minutes to reduce the heat. Transfer the mix to a container, and place in an ice bath, in order to cool the custard as quickly as possible to 4°C.

4 Put a little of the custard in a blender with the brown and white crab meat and the lemon juice, and blend to a purée. Stir the crab purée into the custard; cover the container and put in the fridge to mature for a minimum of 4 hours (or ideally overnight). Strain.

5 Churn in an ice-cream machine until firm or follow the still-freezing method (see page 43). Put in a sealed container and cover the top of the ice cream with waxed or greaseproof paper. Transfer to the freezer until needed.

6 For the sherbet, rinse and dry the sorrel leaves, remove the stalks then put with all the other ingredients in a blender. If you have time, transfer the mix to a covered container in the fridge for a couple of hours for the flavours to develop.

7 Churn in an ice-cream machine until firm or follow the still-freezing method (see page 43). Put in a sealed container and cover the top of the sherbet with waxed or greaseproof paper. Transfer to the freezer until needed.

blue cheese ice cream with pineapple compote

I love the salty, savoury richness of Blue Cheese Ice Cream and serve it with a variety of fruits, such as sliced or poached pears, or simply with some sticks of celery. Pairing Blue Cheese Ice Cream with Pineapple Compote may sound more unusual, but just remind yourself of those canapés so popular in the 1970s – chunks of pineapple and blue cheese on a cocktail stick. The combination of fresh chunks of pineapple stewed in molasses with the sharp, intense flavours of blue cheese really is delicious.

SERVES 10 single scoops (approx. 750 g)

for the ice cream
400 ml whole milk
100 ml whipping cream
3 egg yolks
115 g caster sugar
150 g blue cheese, crumbled (depending on the strength of your blue cheese, more or less may be used)

for the compote
2 pineapples
100 g molasses sugar
20 g unsalted butter

1 For the ice cream, heat the milk and cream in a pan to just below boiling point. Remove from the heat and set aside.

2 Beat the egg yolks with the sugar. Add the warm milk to the egg-sugar mix and return the mixture to the pan. Heat, stirring continuously, to 80°C on a probe thermometer and maintain for 15 seconds. Do not allow the mix to boil or it will scramble.

3 Turn off the heat and continue whisking the mix for a few minutes to reduce the heat. Add the crumbled blue cheese and continue whisking until it is thoroughly incorporated into the custard.

4 Transfer the mix to a container, and place in an ice bath, in order to cool the custard as quickly as possible to 4°C. Once cooled, cover the container and transfer to the fridge to mature for a minimum of 4 hours (or ideally overnight).

5 Churn in an ice-cream machine until firm or follow the still-freezing method (see page 43). Put in a sealed container and cover the top of the ice cream with waxed or greaseproof paper. Transfer to the freezer until needed.

6 For the compote, cut the ends off the pineapples and remove the skin and 'eyes'. Remove and discard the central core. Chop the remaining pineapple flesh into chunks.

7 Put the pineapple chunks into a wide, shallow pan or frying pan with the molasses sugar. Set over a high heat and cook, stirring occasionally, until the sugar has melted.

8 Turn down the heat to low, add the butter and cook gently for 20 minutes, stirring occasionally. Set aside until needed. The compote may be served warm or cold.

gin and tonic sorbet with candied limes

The Gin and Tonic Sorbet is an adaptation of a recipe from the excellent book *Ices: The Definitive Guide* by Caroline Liddell and Robin Weir, which was an invaluable guide for me when I first started making ice cream. The essential difference between this recipe and the one in their book is that I am more profligate with my gin – the consequence of which is that you should be patient with the time it takes to churn, since alcohol depresses the freezing point of the sorbet.

Gin and Tonic Sorbet is probably the most popular sorbet at weddings and civil partnerships (oh, and also at children's parties, where many parents are looking for a little sustenance!).

Please be aware that this is not a very stable sorbet due to the amount of alcohol in it – once it begins to melt on a hot day, it will quickly turn to slush (even if it is stabilised somewhat by the addition of an egg white), so eat fast! *Please note that you will need to prepare the limes by putting them in the freezer the day before you want to serve the sorbet. You will also need a mandolin in order to make the limes, as cutting them finely with a very sharp knife does not yield the same results. This recipe contains raw egg white.*

SERVES 30 shot-glass-sized canapés (approx. 1.2 kg)

for the sorbet
3 tbsp glucose syrup (optional)

500 ml stock syrup (cooled)

350 ml gin

450 ml tonic water

juice of 2 limes, strained

1 egg white (optional)

for the limes
5–6 limes (preferably un-waxed)

100 ml stock syrup

1 Wash and dry the limes and put them in the freezer overnight.

2 For the sorbet, mix all of the ingredients, except for the egg whites, together.

3 Churn in an ice-cream machine or follow the still-freezing method (see page 43) until almost firm, then add the egg white, if using, to the mix and continue churning until the sorbet is firm.

4 Transfer to a sealed container and cover the top of the sorbet with waxed or greaseproof paper. Transfer to the freezer until needed.

5 For the limes, pre-heat the oven to 50°C. Cut the limes across their heads with a sharp knife so that you create a flat surface. Slice the limes on a mandolin, making sure you use the guard to protect your fingers. Do not slice them so thinly that they lose their shape.

7 Put the limes in the syrup and leave them to soak for 5 minutes then put them in an ovenproof dish in the oven. Let them dry in the oven on a low heat until they are crisp. Transfer them to a sheet of non-stick baking paper until needed.

TO SERVE *Scoop the sorbet into shot glasses or onto saucers served with a teaspoon and top with the candied limes. The limes do not need to be perfectly round to be served. They can be served in halves or even just the zest. The point is to evoke the spirit, as it were, of a good old G'n'T!*

TIP *There is no need to add egg white to the sorbet if you don't wish to – it is just that it holds the sorbet together and stabilises it better if you do.*

a sparkling sorbet

Also known as Champagne Sorbet, except that it can be made using any sparkling wine. But bearing in mind the medieval English proverb, ' none can make goodly silke of a gotes fleece' , I wouldn' t try to make this sorbet unless you have purchased something really decent. Remember that as well as some of the Champagne houses, there are some excellent producers of English sparkling wine whose wines quite easily rival those from Champagne, so it is always worth doing your homework.

SERVES 6–7 (approx. 1 kg)

2 tbsp glucose syrup (optional)
500 ml stock syrup, cooled
500 ml sparkling wine
juice of 1 lemon

1 If you are using glucose syrup, heat it in a pan with the stock syrup, stirring, until the glucose syrup has dissolved. Allow to cool.

2 Mix all of the ingredients together and churn in an ice-cream machine until firm or follow the still-freezing method (see page 43).

3 Put in a sealed container and cover the top of the sorbet with waxed or greaseproof paper. Transfer to the freezer until needed.

TIP *This sorbet does not keep and should be consumed on the day it is made.*

cosmopolitan sorbet

Although this can be made using cranberry juice, the cartoned juice is often already sweetened, and so it gives you no control over either the level of sweetness of your sorbet or the intensity of flavour.

In addition, cranberries are highly nutritious and have a high pectin content, so the texture of your sorbet will be much better if you use fresh ones. It is also much more fun to buy fresh cranberries when they become available in the shops in December and hear them crack and pop in your pan as they cook!

SERVES 4 (approx. 800 g)

400 g fresh cranberries
100 ml vodka
200 g caster sugar
a squeeze of fresh lime juice
a squeeze of fresh orange juice

1 Rinse the cranberries then put them into a wide, shallow pan with 400 ml of water, the vodka and the sugar. Bring to just below boiling point and give the cranberries a good stir, then reduce the heat and simmer for approximately 5 minutes or until you hear the cranberries pop. Allow to cool.

2 Put everything in a blender and purée. Strain. Add the lime juice and orange juice. If you have time, put the mix in a covered container in the fridge for a couple of hours to allow the flavours to develop.

3 Churn in an ice-cream machine until firm or follow the still-freezing method (see page 43). Put in a sealed container and cover the top of the sorbet with waxed or greaseproof paper. Transfer to the freezer until needed.

pomegranate royal sorbet

SERVES 6 (approx. 650 g)

4 pomegranates (approx. 250 ml juice)
1 tbsp glucose syrup (optional)
200 ml stock syrup, cooled
250 ml sparkling wine
juice of 2 limes

1 The easiest way to extract the juice from a pomegranate is to roll the fruit on a counter while pressing it firmly in order to release the juice from the seeds. Don't press too hard or you will pierce the flesh. Then hold the fruit over a bowl and puncture it with a fork or small sharp knife, and squeeze the fruit to extract the juice. Strain. Reserve some of the seeds for adding to the sorbet later.

2 If you are using glucose syrup, heat it in a pan with the stock syrup, stirring occasionally, until the glucose dissolves. Cool.

3 Stir the pomegranate juice, sparkling wine and lime juice into the cooled syrup. Churn in an ice-cream machine until firm or follow the still-freezing method (see page 43). Put in a sealed container and cover the top of the sorbet with waxed or greaseproof paper. Transfer to the freezer until needed.

TO **SERVE** *Allow the sorbet to soften then top with the pomegranate seeds.*

TIP *This sorbet does not keep and should be eaten on the day it is made.*

spiced valpolicella and chocolate sorbet

Valpolicella is made primarily from the Corvina, Rondinella and Molinara grapes grown in the Veneto region of Italy. It has a medium to full body with ripe plum and cherry flavours, and a slightly bitter finish. The best producers, primarily in the Classico area, enrich their wines by the process of *ripasso*, re-fermenting the wine with the pomace of Amarone to give it better depth and complexity.

Valpolicella works fabulously with plain chocolate, as they both have fruitiness, bitterness and acidity. However, in the absence of Valpolicella at your local wine merchant, choose a Dolcetto or Salice Salentino. Actually, if you like the idea of pairing red wine with chocolate, any fruity, medium-bodied red wine will do, but Valpolicella really is the perfect partner.

SERVES 5–6 (approx. 850 g)

450 ml Valpolicella
150 g caster sugar
1 cinnamon stick
200 g plain chocolate (min. cocoa solids 70 per cent)

1 Heat the red wine, caster sugar and cinnamon stick in a pan until boiling point, then reduce the heat and let it simmer for 30 minutes. Remove and discard the cinnamon stick.

2 Break the chocolate into pieces and put into a bowl. Whisk in the red wine syrup until thoroughly amalgamated. Add 200 ml of cold water and strain. If you have time, transfer the mix to a covered container in the fridge for a couple of hours to allow the flavours to develop.

3 Churn in an ice-cream machine until firm or follow the still-freezing method (see page 43). Put in a sealed container and cover the top of the sorbet with waxed or greaseproof paper. Transfer to the freezer until needed.

prune and armagnac ice cream

SERVES 8 (approx. 1.2 kg)

150 g caster sugar
100 ml Armagnac
200 g pitted Agen prunes
500 ml whole milk
500 ml double cream
6 egg yolks

1 The day before you intend to make the ice cream, bring 50 ml of water, 50 g of the sugar, the Armagnac and the prunes to a gentle boil in a pan. Turn off the heat and cool, then cover and leave the prunes to swell and infuse in the Armagnac syrup for 24 hours.

2 On the following day, remove approximately six prunes from the mix, chop them roughly and set aside. Put the remaining prune mix into a blender and blitz to a smooth purée.

3 Heat the milk and cream to just below boiling point. Meanwhile, whisk the egg yolks with the remaining sugar, then add the warm milk to the egg mix and return the mixture to the pan. Heat, stirring continuously, to 80°C on a probe thermometer and maintain for 15 seconds. Do not allow the mix to boil or it will scramble.

4 Remove the custard from the heat and continue whisking for a few minutes to reduce the heat , then whisk in the prune and Armagnac purée. Transfer the mix to a container, and place in an ice bath, in order to cool the custard as quickly as possible to 4°C. Cover the container and transfer to the fridge to mature for a minimum of 4 hours (or ideally overnight).

5 Churn in an ice-cream machine until firm or follow the still-freezing method (see page 43) then add the chopped prunes. Put in a sealed container and cover the top of the ice cream with waxed or greaseproof paper. Transfer to the freezer until needed.

nougat ice cream with oranges

In 1986 I was working as a duty manager in Joe Allen restaurant in Covent Garden when my sister arrived with her new boyfriend – a tall, skeletal and somewhat dishevelled chef by the name of Marco Pierre White. I recall him being confident to the point of arrogance and telling me how he was soon going to open a new restaurant in Wandsworth and that it would be famous. Intrigued, I went to see him cooking and was astonished by his skill, his drive and his imaginative flair. He offered me a job as restaurant manager at his new venture, and that is how I came to work at Harvey' s when it opened in 1987. He was right, of course: Harvey' s very soon did become famous, as did Marco. It was my first taste of a 90-hour week and the blood and sweat of aspirational Michelin cooking.

One of Harvey' s most popular and famous desserts was Biscuit Glacé. I have adapted this recipe from *White Heat* by Marco Pierre White; you will need a terrine mould or loaf tin to make it.

This recipe contains raw egg whites.

SERVES 12 (approx. 850 g)

40 g whole blanched almonds
40 g whole blanched hazelnuts
40 g shelled unsalted pistachio nuts
375 g caster sugar
6 egg whites, at room temperature
300 ml whipping cream
4 oranges, to serve

1 Pre-heat the oven to 175°C. Line a baking sheet with non-stick baking paper.

2 Roast the almonds and hazelnuts in an ovenproof dish for approximately 10 minutes. Allow to cool. Combine all the nuts, including the pistachios, and smash them with a rolling pin or pestle into small pieces. Do not let them become powdery.

3 Measure out 115 g of the sugar and put half of it in a pan set over a moderate heat. Stir until the sugar melts; it will become crumbly to begin with, but don't worry. Make sure all the sugar has melted before you add the remaining half of the measured sugar. Scrape the bottom and the sides of the pan as you go along until you have added all 115 g of sugar. Cook the caramel until it turns a lovely golden brown.

4 Add the nuts to the caramel, and stir them around for a few minutes until they are well coated. Pour the praline onto the baking sheet and allow to cool, after which smash into small, rough chunks and set aside.

5 Whisk the egg whites until they are frothy then add the remaining 260 g of the sugar, a little at a time, and continue whisking to make soft peaks. Separately, whisk the cream until it is thick and fold this into the meringue, followed by the praline chunks.

6 Line a loaf tin or terrine with cling film, leaving plenty of overhang. Spoon the nougat into the terrine, and wrap the top in the overhanging cling film. Freeze for a minimum of 6 hours.

TO SERVE *Peel the oranges, removing as much of the pith as possible. Slice the oranges horizontally and arrange 3–4 slices at the top of each serving plate. Cut the terrine of frozen nougat into slices and place below the oranges so that the nougat ice cream is nearest to the guest.*

christmas pudding ice cream with pedro ximénez sherry

This is always a firm favourite with guests at a winter wedding, who cannot quite believe their eyes when they see an ice-cream van pull up outside the church in December! I also always make this ice cream instead of Christmas pudding; it embraces the flavour and spirit of a festive pudding without all of the stodginess.

SERVES 10 generously (approx. 1.6 kg)

250 g mincemeat (look for brands without suet in them as the moistness
   provided by the suet is not required in this instance)
100 ml Pedro Ximénez sherry, plus extra for serving
500 ml whole milk
500 ml whipping cream
9 egg yolks
100 g caster sugar

1 Put the mincemeat in a bowl with the PX sherry, cover and set aside to macerate.

2 Heat the milk and cream in a pan to just below boiling point. Whisk the egg yolks with the sugar. Add the warm milk to the egg–sugar mix and return the mixture to the pan. Heat, stirring continuously, to 80°C on a probe thermometer and maintain for 15 seconds. Do not allow the mix to boil or it will scramble.

3 Remove the custard from the heat and continue whisking for a few minutes to remove some heat, then transfer the mix to a container, and place in an ice bath, in order to cool the custard as quickly as possible to 4°C. Once cooled, cover the container and transfer to the fridge to mature for a minimum of 4 hours (or ideally overnight).

4 Churn in an ice-cream machine or follow the still-freezing method (see page 43) until almost firm, then add the mincemeat mix and continue churning until firm. Put in a sealed container and cover the top of the ice cream with waxed or greaseproof paper. Transfer to the freezer until needed.

zabaglione ice cream

SERVES 5–6 (approx. 850 g)

12 egg yolks
200 g caster sugar
250 ml Marsala
450 ml whipping cream

1 Whisk the egg yolks with the caster sugar.

2 Transfer the mixture to a bowl set over a pan of simmering water, ensuring the hot water does not touch the bowl. Add the Marsala and whisk constantly until the mixture begins to foam and swell into a soft, frothy mass. If you are using a probe thermometer, heat to 80°C and maintain for 15 seconds.

3 Add the cream, then transfer the mix to a container, and place in an ice bath, in order to cool the custard as quickly as possible to 4°C. Put the mix in a covered container and transfer to the fridge to mature for a minimum of 4 hours (or ideally overnight.)

4 Churn in an ice-cream machine until firm or follow the still-freezing method (see page 43), bearing in mind that the alcohol will slow down the freezing process. Put in a sealed container and cover the top of the ice cream with waxed or greaseproof paper. Transfer to the freezer until needed.

hokey pokey ice cream

This is a favourite ice cream in New Zealand – chunks of honeycomb mixed with vanilla ice cream. I have omitted the vanilla pods in this recipe because there is already so much flavour from the honeycomb.

SERVES 10–11 (approx. 1.6 kg)

for the ice cream
750 ml whole milk
450 ml whipping cream
6 egg yolks
100 g caster sugar

for the honeycomb
250 g caster sugar
125 g golden syrup
1 tbsp bicarbonate of soda
butter, for greasing

1 For the ice cream, heat the milk and cream in a pan to just below boiling point. Remove from the heat and set aside.

2 Whisk the egg yolks with the sugar. Add the warm milk to the egg-sugar mix and return the mixture to the pan. Heat the custard, stirring continuously, to 80°C on a probe thermometer and maintain it for 15 seconds. Do not allow the mix to boil or it will scramble.

3 Turn off the heat and continue whisking the custard for a few minutes to remove some heat, then transfer the mix to a container, and place in an ice bath, in order to cool the custard as quickly as possible to 4°C.

4 For the honeycomb, line a shallow baking sheet with waxed or greaseproof paper and butter it (otherwise the honeycomb will stick to the paper). Set aside.

5 Put the caster sugar and the golden syrup into a large, shallow pan, and heat gently, stirring as you go, until everything is dissolved. Turn up the heat and bring to the boil, then reduce the heat and let it simmer for 5–8 minutes. Stir in the bicarbonate of soda. The mixture will bubble and slowly rise to the top of the pan.

6 Pour the honeycomb into the baking sheet and allow it to cool completely and harden. This will take an hour or so, after which bash the honeycomb carefully into chunks with a rolling pin. Put it into an airtight container until needed.

7 Once the ice cream is cool, transfer the custard to a fridge to mature for a minimum of 4 hours or overnight.

8 Churn the custard in an ice-cream machine until almost firm or follow the still-freezing method (see page 43), then add the pieces and crumbs of honeycomb and continue churning until it is firm (you can keep some honeycomb to one side and add it as a topping later, if you wish). Put in a sealed container and cover the top of the ice cream with waxed or greaseproof paper. Transfer to the freezer until needed.

Sundaes

Sundaes, or coupes, are desserts made with scoops of one or more flavours of ice cream, sorbet or sherbet. They were traditionally served in glass or silver cups, hence the French term *coupe*, and are usually served with a sauce and a garnish, such as fruit, biscuits or pastry. I serve my sundaes in all manner of styles, combining tradition with dissent!

Some of the sundaes included in this section are classic recipes, such as Concorde and Cardinal, while others are a play on time-honoured combinations, such as Poire Belle Hélène. Others are ' deconstructions' of a particular dish and work within a frozen context because they still maintain the principle of ingredients that empirically work well together, albeit placed into a dessert context.

All of the recipes can be made as stand-alones, if you prefer not to combine them as suggested.

peach melba   serves 4

Vanilla ice cream · Raspberry sauce · Poached peaches

A classic sundae, created in honour of the soprano Dame Nellie Melba by Escoffier. The combination of plump peaches poached in their syrup and topped with vanilla ice cream and fresh raspberry sauce is as irresistible now as it must have been to Dame Nellie (and how lovely to have had Escoffier as a friend!).

Vanilla Ice Cream (see page 53)
Raspberry Sauce (see page 204)

for the peaches
1 vanilla pod
100 g sugar
zest of 1 lemon
4 peaches

1 Split the vanilla pod in half lengthways and scrape out the seeds. Put 500 ml of water into a saucepan together with the sugar, the vanilla pod and its seeds and the lemon zest and bring to a boil. Reduce the heat and simmer for 5 minutes to reduce the liquid so that it is slightly viscous. Wash the peaches and cut them in half. Place them in the sugar syrup and let them poach gently in the liquid for approximately 5 minutes, then turn them over and continue poaching for a further 5 minutes (poaching time will vary according to how ripe the peaches are; I have sometimes had to double this time). Test to see if they are done by inserting a knife into them; if the knife does not penetrate easily, then they need poaching a little longer. Turn off the heat and let them cool in their syrup.

2 Remove the skins and stones from the peaches and discard. Transfer the peaches and their poaching syrup into a sealed container and store in the fridge until needed.

TO SERVE PEACH MELBA *Allow the vanilla ice cream to soften a little. Place two scoops of vanilla ice cream into a coupe glass or regular glass bowl. Slice the peach halves into two and place them on top of the ice cream, together with a little of their poaching syrup. Spoon the raspberry sauce on top. If you have kebab skewers, put four slices of peach onto each skewer, then dig the skewer into the vanilla ice cream before spooning the sauce over it.*

five tastes of japan   serves 6

Japanese red bean ice cream · Sweet miso ice cream · Green tea ice cream · Seaweed 'fior di latte' · Pickled ginger compote

This sundae explores the concept of the five 'taste sensations' – sweet, sour, salty, bitter and 'umami' – in a dessert context. In Asia, umami is considered to be the fifth taste and is used to describe the perception of savouriness, which is distinct from the other four tastes and is commonly associated with protein-rich foods such as meat, fish and cheese, and some vegetables.

In this sundae, Japanese Red Bean Ice Cream illustrates sweetness; Green Tea Ice Cream illustrates bitter; the salty taste comes from Sweet Miso Ice Cream, and the Pickled Ginger Compote gives you sour. Finding a flavour that illustrated umami in an ice cream proved to be far more difficult, short of making an ice cream from Wagyu Kobe beef! I experimented with various Japanese ingredients, including a dipping sauce for noodles called Yamasa zarusoba senka, which contains bonito flakes. This gave a pretty good perception of savouriness, though it did not really work in an ice cream. My own preference for illustrating the concept of umami is Parmesan Ice Cream (see page 155), except Parmesan, of course, is not Japanese. I have therefore included a very simple combination of milk, sugar and kombu (a Japanese kelp) which I churn into an ice cream (or iced milk, to be exact). A Japanese academic first started to experiment with kombu in 1907 in order to try and identify the taste of umami, and extracted crystals of glutamic acid, which is a building block for protein and is present in flavours associated with umami. It is therefore a good example of the concept of savouriness.

Japanese red bean ice cream

There are two ways to make this ice cream – the hard way and the easy way. The hard way starts off easily – pop down to the local store and pick up a bag of adzuki beans. Then the laborious process of pre-soaking and simmering for hours commences. The easy way is only easy if you have a Japanese or specialist store nearby, in which case buy a can of yude adzuki (boiled and sweetened red beans) and avoid having to prepare the beans yourself. The former will make you feel virtuous; the latter will make you feel clever.

SERVES 6–7 single scoops (approx. 500 g)

for the beans
200 g prepared boiled red beans
    or 100 g dried adzuki beans
75 g caster sugar
a squeeze of lemon

for the custard mix
125 ml whole milk
125 ml whipping cream
50 g caster sugar
2 egg yolks

1 If you are making the ice cream from dried adzuki beans, put them in a bowl of water and leave to soak overnight.

2 On the following day, drain the beans and give them a good rinse. Put the beans into a pan with 1,25 l water, the caster sugar and the lemon juice. Bring to the boil and boil rapidly for 10 minutes, then reduce the heat and simmer for 2–3 hours or until the beans are completely tender. (If you need to add more water because the beans are not tender enough, do so.)

3 While the beans are cooking, make the custard. Put the milk and cream into a pan and heat to just below boiling point. Beat the egg yolks with the sugar. Add the warm milk to the egg-sugar mix and return the mixture to the pan. Heat, stirring continuously, to 80°C on a probe thermometer and maintain for 15 seconds. Do not allow the mix to boil or it will scramble.

4 Turn off the heat and continue whisking the mix for a few minutes to reduce the heat then transfer the mix to a container, and place in an ice bath, in order to cool the custard as quickly as possible to 4°C. Once cooled, cover the container and transfer to the fridge to mature for a minimum of 4 hours (or ideally overnight).

5 When the dried beans are tender, drain the water: you should have roughly 200 g of beans and liquid together. If there is much more than that due to excess liquid, discard some, leaving 200 g. Put the beans and liquid into a blender and pulverise.

6 Blend the adzuki bean mix into the custard. If you have bought the tinned adzuki beans, now blend these with the custard. Churn in an ice-cream machine until firm or follow the still-freezing method (see page 43). Put in a sealed container and cover the top of the ice cream with waxed or greaseproof paper. Transfer to the freezer until needed.

Sweet miso ice cream

This is an adaptation of pastry chef Sam Mason's recipe from the New York restaurant wd~50. The saltiness of sweet white miso works really well against the sweetness and creaminess of the custard mix.

SERVES 6 single scoops (approx. 450 g)

250 ml whole milk
125 ml whipping cream
75 g caster sugar
3 egg yolks
75 g sweet white miso

1 Heat the milk and cream in a pan to just below boiling point.

2 Beat the egg yolks with the sugar. Add the warm milk to the egg-sugar mix and return the mixture to the pan. Heat the custard, stirring continuously, to 80°C on a probe thermometer and maintain for 15 seconds. Do not allow the mix to boil or it will scramble.

3 Turn off the heat and continue whisking the custard for a few minutes to reduce the heat. Whisk in the sweet white miso then transfer the mix to a container, and place in an ice bath, in order to cool the custard as quickly as possible to 4°C. Once cooled, cover the container and transfer to the fridge to mature for a minimum of 4 hours (or ideally overnight).

4 Churn in an ice-cream machine until firm or follow the still-freezing method (see page 43). Put in a sealed container and cover the top of the ice cream with waxed or greaseproof paper. Transfer to the freezer until needed.

Green tea ice cream

SERVES 6–7 single scoops (approx. 500 g)

350 ml whole milk
125 ml whipping cream
5 g Matcha (green tea powder) (about 1–2 level teaspoons)
180 g caster sugar
2 egg yolks

1 Put the milk and cream into a pan and heat to just below boiling point. Put the green tea powder into a saucer and add a small amount of boiling water to make a paste. Whisk the paste into the warmed milk.

2 Beat the egg yolks with the sugar. Add the warm milk to the egg–sugar mix and return the mixture to the pan. Heat, stirring continuously, to 80°C on a probe thermometer and maintain for 15 seconds. Do not allow the mix to boil or it will scramble.

3 Turn off the heat and continue whisking the mix for a few minutes to reduce the heat. Transfer the mix to a container, and place in an ice bath, in order to cool the custard as quickly as possible to 4˚C. Once cooled, cover the container and transfer to the fridge to mature for a minimum of 4 hours (or ideally overnight).

4 Churn in an ice-cream machine or follow the still-freezing method (see page 43). Put in a sealed container and cover the top of the ice cream with waxed or greaseproof paper. Transfer to the freezer until needed.

Seaweed 'fior di latte'

Fior di latte ('flower of milk') is a simple ice cream made from milk, cream and sugar. I have used the term a little loosely (and my apologies to the purists), because it is not normally accompanied by flavouring and is a simple combination of the three ingredients. In this combination, the sweetness of the dairy comes through on the front palate followed by the earthy flavours of kombu.

SERVES 6–7 single scoops (approx. 500 g)

2 sheets dried kombu
500 ml whole milk
125 g caster sugar

1 Wipe the sheets of kombu with a cloth and put in a pan with the milk. Let the kombu hydrate for 15 minutes.

2 Heat the milk and sugar to just below boiling point, then turn the heat off and cool. Strain the milk. Discard the kombu.

3 Churn in an ice-cream machine until firm or follow the still-freezing method (see page 43). Put in a sealed container and cover with waxed or greaseproof paper. Transfer to the freezer until needed.

Pickled ginger compote

120 g pickled ginger
25 g caster sugar

1 Strain the pickled ginger and discard the liquid.

2 Heat the sugar and 50 ml of water in a pan to boiling point. Turn off the heat, add the pickled ginger and rest for 5 minutes. Strain and discard the syrup. Allow to cool. Set aside until needed.

TO SERVE FIVE TASTES OF JAPAN *Allow the ice creams to soften a little. Place a spoonful of each in a bowl with the Pickled Ginger Compote on the side. An alternative way of serving this sundae is to present it 'sushi-style'. Spoon a tablespoon of each ice cream onto small dishes set on a large plate. Tablespoon sizes are obviously much smaller than regular scoop sizes, so halving the recipe of each ice cream will give you plenty for a party of 12, with some left over.*

flavours of the far east serves 10

Lemon grass ice cream · Pineapple and chilli sorbet · Szechuan
peppercorn ice cream · Coconut and kaffir lime leaf sorbet

This sundae is a combination of 'Asian' flavours: there's the punch of the
Pineapple and Chilli Sorbet and the Szechuan Peppercorn Ice Cream set
against the cooling, mellow flavours of the Lemon Grass Ice Cream and the
Coconut and Kaffir Lime Leaf Sorbet.

Lemon grass ice cream

When selecting lemon grass, choose fresh-looking stalks that don't seem dry or
brittle. Lemon grass can be stored in the fridge in a tightly sealed plastic bag for
up to 3 weeks without any loss of flavour. Lemon grass contains citral, the active
ingredient in lemon peel, but its flavours are much softer, less aggressive and more
aromatic than lemon.

SERVES 10–11 single scoops (approx. 800 g)

5 lemon grass stalks
600 ml whole milk
125 ml whipping cream
125 g caster sugar
   or 110 g caster sugar and 1 tbsp glucose syrup
4 kaffir lime leaves
3 egg yolks

1 Rinse the lemon grass, remove the ends and the tough outer leaves, then bruise
the remaining stalks with a pestle and mortar or rolling pin and roughly chop.

2 Heat the lemon grass in a pan with the milk, cream, glucose syrup (if using)
and kaffir lime leaves to just below boiling point. Remove from the heat and allow
the ingredients to infuse for an hour.

3 Strain the mix and discard the lemon grass and lime leaves. Return the milk to
a pan and reheat. In the meantime, whisk the egg yolks with the sugar. Add the
warm milk to the egg-sugar mix and return the mixture to the pan. Heat, stirring

continuously, to 80°C on a probe thermometer and maintain for 15 seconds. Do not allow the mix to boil or it will scramble.

4 Remove the custard from the heat and continue whisking for a few minutes to remove some heat Transfer the mix to a container, and place in an ice bath, in order to cool the custard as quickly as possible to 4°C. Once cooled, cover the container and transfer to the fridge to mature for a minimum of 4 hours (or ideally overnight).

5 Churn in an ice-cream machine until firm or follow the still-freezing method (see page 43). Put in a sealed container and cover the top of the ice cream with waxed or greaseproof paper. Transfer to the freezer until needed.

Pineapple and chilli sorbet

SERVES 12 single scoops (approx. 900 g)

2 red chillies
1 tbsp glucose syrup (optional)
250 ml stock syrup
1 large pineapple (approx. 700 g flesh)
juice of half a lime

1 Wash and dry the chillies, seed them and chop them finely. Discard the seeds.

2 If using glucose syrup, heat it in a pan with the stock syrup until it dissolves. Turn off the heat. Add the chopped chillies and infuse in the syrup for 15 minutes.

3 Slice the top and bottom off the pineapple, remove the skin and any ' eyes' with a sharp knife and remove and discard the inner core. Chop the flesh into chunks. Put everything in a blender and blend till smooth. Put the mix in a covered container and transfer to the fridge for a couple of hours to allow the flavours to develop.

4 Churn in an ice-cream machine until firm or follow the still-freezing method (see page 43). Put the sorbet in to a sealed container and cover the top of the sorbet with waxed or greaseproof paper. Transfer to the freezer until needed.

Szechuan peppercorn ice cream

Szechuan peppercorns, also known as flower pepper, fagara or Japanese pepper, aren't actually peppercorns at all; they are the berries from a small, prickly ash tree. They are aromatic and slightly citrusy; if dry roasted for a few minutes, they release their aromatics and give a lovely, soft pungency to the ice cream.

SERVES 10–11 single scoops (approx. 800 g)

20 g Szechuan peppercorns
500 ml whole milk
200 ml whipping cream
6 egg yolks
180 g caster sugar
  or 165 g caster sugar and 1 tbsp glucose syrup

1 Dry roast the peppercorns on the stove for a couple of minutes until they start to smoke. Stir them around so that they don't burn.

2 Heat the milk, cream, glucose syrup, if using, and the peppercorns in a pan to just below boiling point. Take off the heat and infuse for 15 minutes. Strain the mix through a chinois or regular sieve, discard the peppercorns then return the milk and cream to the pan.

3 In the meantime, whisk the egg yolks with the sugar. Add the warm milk to the egg-sugar mix and return the mixture to the pan. Heat, stirring continuously, to 80°C on a probe thermometer and maintain for 15 seconds. Do not allow the mix to boil or it will scramble.

4 Remove the custard from the heat and continue whisking for a few minutes until it loses some heat. Transfer to a container that can be placed on an ice bath to cool the custard as rapidly as possible to 4°C. Cover the container and transfer to a fridge to mature for a minimum of 4 hours or overnight.

5 Churn in an ice-cream machine until firm or follow the still-freezing method (see page 43). Put in a sealed container and cover the top of the ice cream with waxed or greaseproof paper. Transfer to the freezer until needed.

Coconut and kaffir lime leaf sorbet

SERVES 12 single scoops (approx. 900 g)

750 ml coconut milk
3 kaffir lime leaves
1 tbsp glucose syrup (optional)
175 ml stock syrup
juice of half a lime

1 Heat the coconut milk, kaffir lime leaves, glucose syrup, if using, and stock syrup in a pan to just below boiling point. Take off the heat and allow the lime leaves to infuse for 15 minutes.

2 Strain and discard the lime leaves. Cool then add the lime juice. If you have time, cover the container and put it in the fridge for a couple of hours for the flavours to mature.

3 Churn in an ice-cream machine until firm or follow the still-freezing method (see page 43). Put in a sealed container and cover the top of the sorbet with waxed or greaseproof paper. Transfer to the freezer until needed.

TO SERVE FLAVOURS OF THE FAR EAST *If you would like your guests to taste these ices in a particular order, so that they get the best of the contrasting flavours, put a scoop of each in a row on a plate starting from left to right with the Lemon Grass Ice Cream, the Szechuan Peppercorn Ice Cream, followed by the Pineapple and Chilli Sorbet and finally the Coconut and Kaffir Lime Leaf Sorbet.*

dolci tricolore   serves 12–14

Basil and buffalo milk ice cream · Tomato granita · Olive oil gelato ·
Balsamic snaps · Candied basil

As buffalo milk is now available in many farmers' markets, I thought it would be
fun to create a sundae based around 'insalata tricolore', a classic salad that
mimics the colours of the Italian flag, usually containing buffalo mozzarella,
tomatoes and basil. The ingredients work well when combined both in a savoury
and in a dessert context. You do not need to use buffalo milk for the Basil and
Buffalo Milk Ice Cream, however, and can substitute milk from another animal
(if using cows' milk, substitute a third of the milk quantity with single cream).

Basil and buffalo milk ice cream

I regard this as more of an 'iced milk' than an ice cream; I add gelatine to the mix in
order to give it some texture. (If you are vegetarian, substitute the gelatine for 2
tablespoons of glucose syrup.) The ice-cream mix needs to be churned then put into a
terrine mould or loaf tin and transferred to the freezer for a few hours to freeze well
enough that it can be sliced to look like mozzarella on the plate. If you are not bothered
by the 'mozzarella' look, just freeze and churn the ice cream in the usual manner.

SERVES 12–14 slices (approx. 1 kg)

3 leaves gelatine
1 litre buffalo milk
175 g caster sugar
40 g fresh basil leaves

1   Put the leaves of gelatine into a bowl of cold water and leave for about 5
minutes to swell. In the meantime, heat the buffalo milk in a pan with the sugar.
Once the gelatine has swollen up, squeeze out as much of the water as possible
then add the leaves to the warmed milk, and stir until they dissolve.

2   Wash the basil leaves and add them, with their stalks, to the milk then heat to
80°C on a probe thermometer and maintain for 15 seconds. (This is especially
important if the buffalo milk is unpasteurised, as is often the case.) Allow to cool.

3 Put the mix through a sieve and discard the basil leaves, then put it in a covered container in the fridge to mature for a minimum of 4 hours of overnight.

4 Churn in an ice-cream machine until firm or follow the still-freezing method (see page 43). Line a terrine mould or loaf tin with cling film so that it overhangs, then put the ice cream into it and wrap the overhanging cling film over the top. Put in the freezer for about $1^{1}/2$ hours for the ice cream to set in the mould.

TIP *When you first sample this ice cream, it will taste a little 'icy' because it does not have the richness of a regular ice cream. Although buffalo milk has almost twice the fat content of cows' milk, it still has a much lower fat content than dairy cream. After 10 minutes or so, it will soften a little, and the flavours will come through.*

Tomato granita

SERVES 12–14 (approx. 900 g)

1 kg tomatoes
approx. 15–20 fresh basil leaves
200 ml stock syrup
a squeeze of lemon
salt

1 Wash the tomatoes and blitz in a blender with the basil and a pinch of salt. Put the pulp through a chinois or sieve to extract the juice and some pulp.

2 Combine the juice with the stock syrup and a squeeze of lemon, to taste. Transfer to a covered container in the freezer.

3 When, after about an hour, the mixture begins to form crystals, stir with a fork, ensuring that you scrape down the sides and everything is combined. Return the container to the freezer.

4 Remove and repeat this procedure every half an hour or so until the mixture resembles crushed ice – this may take up to 3 hours.

Olive oil gelato

This requires the freshest and most expensive olive oil you can afford. You will really be able to taste it in the recipe so don't scrimp on quality, if possible.

SERVES 12–14 (approx. 975 g)

750 ml whole milk
zest of 1 unwaxed lemon
9 egg yolks
115 g caster sugar
115 ml extra virgin olive oil

1 Heat the milk and the lemon zest in a pan to just below boiling point. Allow the lemon zest to infuse in the milk for 15 minutes then discard.

2 Whisk the egg yolks with the sugar. Add the warm milk to the egg mix and return the mixture to the pan. Heat, stirring continuously, to 80°C on a probe thermometer and maintain for 15 seconds. Do not allow the mix to boil or it will scramble.

3 Remove the custard from the heat and continue whisking for a few minutes to reduce the heat. Transfer the mix to a container and place in an ice bath, in order to cool the custard as quickly as possible to 4°C. Add the olive oil, whisking it thoroughly until it is amalgamated. Place in a sealed container and transfer to a fridge to mature for a minimum of 4 hours (or ideally overnight).

4 Churn in an ice-cream machine until firm or follow the still-freezing method (see page 43). Put in a sealed container and cover the top of the ice cream with waxed or greaseproof paper. Transfer to the freezer until needed.

Balsamic snaps

60 g caster sugar
60 ml balsamic vinegar
60 g unsalted butter
30 g plain flour, sifted

1 Pre-heat the oven to 180°C. Line a baking sheet with buttered foil or non-stick baking paper.

2 Heat half the sugar in a pan and stir until the sugar dissolves. Add the remaining sugar and repeat, then add the balsamic vinegar followed by the butter. Stir in the flour until everything is incorporated. Remove from the heat then stir the flour, a little at a time, into the mix. Set aside for 15 minutes to rest.

3 Scoop teaspoonfuls of the caramel onto the baking sheet. The balls of caramel will spread into each other as they cook but that does not matter. Bake for approximately 10 minutes or until the caramel is bubbling and golden.

4 Remove from the oven and cool for a couple of minutes, then lift off the 'sheet' of balsamic caramel and, while still pliable, break it into uneven chunks about the size of your palm. Put the balsamic snaps on a clean sheet of foil or non-stick baking paper and allow to cool completely. Store in an airtight container until needed.

Candied basil

fresh basil leaves, allow 5 per person
icing sugar, for dipping

1 Wash and partially dry the basil leaves. Dip the leaves in a bowl of icing sugar. Set the leaves on a sheet of foil and rub the sugar into the leaves with a finger so that they look white. Set aside till needed.

TO SERVE DOLCI TRICOLORE *Allow the the ice creams and granita to soften for serving. (The Olive Oil Gelato takes longest, followed by the Tomato Granita, followed by the Basil and Buffalo Milk Ice Cream. Put the candied basil leaves on each serving plate in whatever decorative style takes your fancy. Put a slice of Basil and Buffalo Milk Ice Cream on the plate and scatter the tomato granita over it. Put a Balsamic Snap onto the plate next to the Basil and Buffalo Milk Ice Cream and place a scoop of Olive Oil Gelato on top.*

poire belle hélène · serves 4

Vanilla ice cream · Pear sorbet · Poached pears · Chocolate sauce · Poire William jelly

This is a slightly more complicated adaptation of the classic, but when pears are in season, why not go all the way and buy a big bagful and poach half of them then make the other half into a sorbet? As for the Poire William Jelly, well, this takes the pear theme one step further, so that you have a three-way pear thing going on. You could, of course, omit the sorbet and jelly, and follow the traditional route of simply poaching the pears and serving them with the Chocolate Sauce and Vanilla Ice Cream.

Vanilla Ice Cream (see page 53)

Pear sorbet

SERVES 4 (approx. 600 g)

600 g ripe pears, peeled and cored
50 g caster sugar
zest of 1 lime plus 2 tsp juice
1 tbsp glucose syrup (optional)

1 Put the pears and put into a wide, shallow pan along with the sugar, 350 ml of water and the lime zest. Bring to just below boiling point, then reduce the heat to a simmer, add the glucose syrup, if using, and allow the pears to poach gently for 15 minutes.

2 Allow to cool. Discard the zest, add the lime juice and purée the mix in a blender. Strain. Churn in an ice-cream machine until firm or follow the still-freezing method (see page 43). Put in a sealed container and cover the top of the sorbet with waxed or greaseproof paper. Transfer to the freezer until needed.

Poached pears

100 g caster sugar
juice and zest of 1 lemon
1 vanilla pod
4 ripe pears (Roca or Comice are good)

1 Split the vanilla pod and remove its seeds. In a wide, shallow pan, heat 400 ml of water with the sugar, the vanilla pod and its seeds and a strip of lemon zest to just below boiling point.

2 In the meantime, peel the pears and rub in a squeeze of lemon juice to prevent discolouration. If you have a corer, core the pears from the base and keep the fruit whole. Alternatively, do not core but keep the fruit whole anyway and leave the stalks on. Place the pears into the poaching syrup, reduce the heat to simmering and poach the pears until they are tender, turning occasionally. This will take approximately 30 minutes, but may take longer if the pears are not very ripe.

3 Allow the pears to cool in the poaching liquid, then transfer both the pears and liquid to a covered container and place in the fridge until needed.

Chocolate sauce

100 g plain chocolate (min. cocoa solids 70 per cent),
   broken into small pieces
150 ml whipping cream
50 ml stock syrup (from the poached pears)

1 Put the chocolate in a bowl set over a pan of simmering water and stir until it melts. Stir in the whipping cream plus 50 ml of the reserved pear syrup. (If you are just making chocolate sauce without poaching pears, use a regular stock syrup.)

2 Put in a covered container and transfer to the fridge until needed.

Poire William jelly

100 ml Poire William liqueur
2 leaves of gelatine
icing sugar, for dusting

1 Heat the Poire William in a pan to just below boiling point. Remove from the heat and allow it to cool for a couple of minutes.

2 Put the gelatine in a bowl and gradually pour the Poire William onto the gelatine (not the other way around) until it has dissolved. Whisk thoroughly.

3 Transfer the mix to an ice-cube tray and allow to set. Once set, remove from the ice tray and cover until needed.

TO SERVE POIRE BELLE HÉLÈNE *If you are serving the Chocolate Sauce hot, then reheat it in a container set over a pan of simmering water. Allow the Vanilla Ice Cream and Pear Sorbet to soften a little. Put one poached pear per person onto a serving plate with a little of the poaching liquid. Add a scoop of Vanilla Ice Cream on one side and a scoop of Pear Sorbet on the other. Spoon Chocolate Sauce over the pear and Vanilla Ice Cream. Dust the Poire William Jelly with a little icing sugar and put it on the edge of the plate.*

a kind of eton mess serves 6

Vanilla ice cream · Tarragon meringue · Spiced strawberries ·
Raspberry sauce

Every year, on the last Wednesday in May, Housemaster Roland Martin and
his wife Kerri, invite me to bring my ice-cream van to Jourdelay's, Eton
College, to take part in the Fourth of June celebrations. One of Eton's best-
known celebrations, it marks the birthday of King George III. I love arriving
at Eton and feeling the flourish of history and occasion.

Eton Mess originated in Eton, from boys' 'Messing' and consists of
strawberries with meringue and cream or ice cream. While I would never
consider deviating from tradition for the Fourth of June celebrations, on this
occasion I have taken the theme of Eton Mess a little sideways, by flavouring
the meringue with tarragon and spicing up the strawberries. If you want a
good old-fashioned classic, simply omit the tarragon from the meringue.
Please note that the meringues are made the day before they are needed.

Very Creamy Vanilla Ice Cream (see page 54)

Tarragon meringue

110 g caster sugar
60 g egg whites (approx. 2 eggs)
10 g fresh tarragon leaves

1 Pre-heat the oven to 150°C. Prepare a baking sheet with non-stick baking paper.

2 In a small pan, bring some water to the boil, then reduce the heat to a simmer.
Put the sugar and egg whites into a bowl and set the bowl over the pan of
simmering water; stir, and let it all dissolve. The mixture should be quite warm.
Whisk the mixture, preferably with an electric hand whisk or mixer, until it is thick
and glossy.

3 Wash and dry the tarragon then cut into very thin strips. Stir into the meringue.
Spoon the meringue onto the non-stick baking paper. This does not need to be done
tidily as the meringue will be broken up later anyway. Put the baking sheet in the
oven then turn off the oven and leave the meringues to dry out overnight.

Spiced strawberries

1 star anise
1 cardamom pod
2 g black peppercorns (approx. 20–25)
400–450 g strawberries
50 ml stock syrup, cold

1 Crush the spices and peppercorns with a pestle and mortar. Remove and discard the cardamom pod, leaving behind the seeds.

2 Wash and hull the strawberries and slice in half lengthways (or into quarters if the strawberries are large).

3 Put the strawberries into a bowl with the crushed spices and stock syrup. Leave to infuse for half an hour, then put the mix into a sieve and discard most of the syrup, leaving a little behind with which to coat the strawberries.

Raspberry sauce

450 g fresh raspberries
50 ml stock syrup, cold

1 Wash the raspberries and put into a blender with the stock syrup. Purée until smooth. Strain to remove the seeds. Cover and keep in the fridge until needed.

TO SERVE A KIND OF ETON MESS *Allow the Very Creamy Vanilla Ice Cream to soften then put two scoops into a bowl. Break the Tarragon Meringue into pieces and arrange around the ice cream. Spoon the Spiced Strawberries on top and the Raspberry Sauce on top of the strawberries.*

glacé de la martinique   serves 6

'Banana milkshake' ice cream . Rum baba . Tamarind and ginger crème chantilly

If Jeremy and Fiona Day, longstanding regulars at Lola's, were amused when I first told them about my ice-cream van, they cannily disguised the smirk on their faces. Once the sniggering had ceased, Jeremy volunteered to help me re-paint the van, then joined me in the kitchens at Lola's and helped me make my first batch of ice cream. A long-term enthusiast of the Caribbean, he suggested I put together a sundae based around Caribbean-style flavours, so I did.

This is my own adaptation of Glacé de la Martinique, which I hope captures the spirit of the sundae.

'Banana milkshake' ice cream

This is an adaptation of Thomas Keller's Poached Banana Ice Cream from his fabulous and challenging *The French Laundry Cookbook*. The bananas are discarded once they have been poached, leaving an infusion that tastes just like a banana milk shake!

SERVES 6–7 single scoops (approx. 500 g)

1 vanilla pod
375 ml whole milk
75 ml whipping cream
100 g caster sugar
  or 85 g caster sugar and 1 tbsp glucose syrup
4 ripe bananas, sliced
3 egg yolks

1 Split the vanilla pod in half and scrape out the seeds.

2 Place the milk, cream, half the sugar, the glucose syrup, if using, vanilla pod and its seeds and the bananas into a pan and cover with a piece of non-stick baking paper in order to keep them submerged. Heat on a very low heat for 10–15 minutes. Do not allow to simmer – the bananas should poach gently. Test the bananas to see if they are soft. Remove from the heat before they turn mushy. Discard the paper and vanilla pod.

3 Strain the milk, reserving it for later. Discard the bananas (or make them into a smoothie).

4 Beat the egg yolks with the remaining sugar. Put the strained milk back into a pan and heat it to just below boiling point. Add the banana milk to the egg mix and return the mixture to the pan. Heat, stirring continuously, to 80°C on a probe thermometer and maintain for 15 seconds. Do not allow the mix to boil or it will scramble.

5 Take the pan off the heat and continue whisking the mix for a few minutes to reduce the heat Transfer the mix to a container, and place in an ice bath, in order to cool the custard as quickly as possible to 4°C. Once cooled, cover the container and transfer to the fridge to mature for a minimum of 4 hours (or ideally overnight).

6 Churn the ice cream until it is firm or follow the still-freezing method (see page 43). Put in a sealed container and cover the top of the ice cream with waxed or greaseproof paper. Transfer to the freezer until needed.

Rum Baba

You will need six 15 cm savarin moulds – these are shallow, tubular moulds. If you do not have these at hand, use dariole moulds.

SERVES 6

for the baba
60 g currants
75 ml dark rum
2 tbsp grated lemon zest
40 ml whole milk
10 g fast-action dried yeast
220 g caster sugar
180 g plain flour
3 large eggs
60 g unsalted butter, plus a little for buttering
a pinch of salt

1 Combine the currants, rum and lemon zest. Set aside. Warm the milk in a pan and then combine with the yeast and 20 g of the sugar in a bowl. Set aside for 5 minutes.

2 Sift the flour and add to the bowl with the salt. Lightly beat the eggs and add these to the bowl. Melt the butter and add this to the mix. Beat well for about 5 minutes until you have a smooth and elastic dough. Cover the bowl and leave in a warm place for approximately 45 minutes–1 hour, or until the dough has doubled in volume.

3 Drain the currants and fold them into the dough. Beat again. Reserve the rum for adding to the syrup later.

4 Butter the savarin moulds and fill each one half full with the dough and prove for a further 45 minutes–1 hour or until the dough has doubled in volume.

5 Heat the oven to 190°C. Bake the babas for 20–25 minutes until risen and golden.

6 Put the remaining 200g of sugar and 100 ml of water in a pan and bring to the boil, then boil rapidly for 5 minutes. Cool a little then add the reserved rum.

7 Allow the babas to cool a little, then turn them out of their moulds and, while still warm, pour over the warm rum syrup so that they are soaked. Set aside until needed.

Tamarind and ginger crème chantilly

150 g whipping cream
75 g caster sugar
1^1/$_2$ heaped tsp tamarind paste
3 tsp stem ginger syrup

1 Whip together all of the ingredients until the cream has doubled in volume and has formed soft peaks. Put in a covered container in the fridge until needed.

TO SERVE GLACÉ DE LA MARTINIQUE *Allow the ice cream to soften a little. Put the Rum Baba on a plate and top it with a scoop of 'Banana Milkshake' Ice Cream followed by a dollop of the Crème Chantilly. If you would like, serve a split banana on the side.*

black and white serves 8

Greek yoghurt ice cream · Sardinian rice gelato nero

I wanted to make a sundae that was very simply 'black and white'. I tried various ways of getting a black ice cream (omitting, of course, the option of a synthetic colouring), but my liquorice ice cream came out a muddy brown. Then I thought of the wonderful dish 'risotto nero' – risotto flavoured with squid ink – and wondered if it would be possible and, in a culinary sense, permissible, to make an ice cream with squid ink.

My former business partner, Carol George, always told me how fond she was of Sardinian rice gelato, which contains rice in the ice cream, so it seemed, from my perspective, a logical leap to put the two together. The black ice cream does not actually taste overtly fishy, rather, it's like a black, frozen rice pudding, with a very subtle hint of squid flavour in the background. The Greek yoghurt ice is a foil for the richness of the former.

Greek yoghurt ice cream

This was another Lola's favourite, brought to us by Juliet Peston. If you don't want to add cream, replace it with the same quantity of Greek yoghurt.

SERVES 8 single scoops (approx. 600 g)

125 ml double cream
500 ml Greek yoghurt
125 g caster sugar
juice of half a lemon

1 Mix everything together in a bowl. Churn in an ice-cream machine until firm or follow the still-freezing method (see page 43).

2 Put into a sealed container and cover the top of the ice cream with waxed or greaseproof paper. Transfer to the freezer until needed.

Sardinian rice gelato nero

This recipe contains raw egg whites.

SERVES 9 single scoops (approx. 700 g)

500 ml whole milk
100 g caster sugar
3 strips of lemon zest
75 g arborio, carnaroli or vialone nano rice
200 ml squid ink
3 egg whites
salt

1 Combine the milk, sugar and lemon zest in a pan and bring to just below boiling point. Reduce the heat; add the rice and simmer, stirring regularly, until the rice is cooked. Check regularly – the rice should still have some resistance when you bite into it, just beyond al dente.

2 Discard the lemon zest and add the squid ink. Transfer to a container that can be placed in an ice bath to cool the mix as rapidly as possible to 4°C.

3 Churn the rice mix in an ice-cream machine till almost firm. Whip the egg whites with a pinch of salt until they form soft peaks. Fold the egg whites into the rice mix and continue churning until firm.

4 Put in a sealed container and cover the top of the ice cream with waxed or greaseproof paper. Transfer to the freezer until needed.

TO SERVE BLACK AND WHITE *Allow both ice creams to soften a little, then place a scoop of each into a bowl, preferably glass as this will have more of a visual effect. Alternatively, and if you are inclined to be controversial (which you probably are in any case just by making this sundae), place a heaped tablespoonful of each ice cream into oyster shells (that have been boiled), adding a teaspoon on the side, and serve as a post-buffet dessert canapé.*

coupe citron   serves 9

Tangerine sorbet · Lime and chocolate sorbet · Cats' tongues

This is essentially a winter sundae, perfect for when the season brings with it its crop of juicy tangerines, satsumas and mandarins. It is a lovely combination of the vibrant, punchy flavours of the Lime and Chocolate Sorbet, the sweet, tangy Tangerine Sorbet and delicately flavoured, soft, textured biscuits.

Tangerine sorbet

SERVES 9 single scoops (approx. 700 g)

12–14 tangerines or satsumas
1 tbsp glucose syrup (optional)
150 ml stock syrup
1–2 tbsp fresh lemon juice (to taste)

1 Juice the tangerines/satsumas then strain, extracting as much of the juice and pulp as possible. Measure out 600 ml.

2 If using glucose syrup, combine it with the stock syrup in a pan and heat till the syrup dissolves. Allow to cool.

3 Combine the stock syrup with the tangerine and lemon juice (the tangerines/satsumas will vary in sweetness but adding the lemon juice will give them a little acidity).

4 Churn in an ice-cream machine until firm or follow the still-freezing method (see page 43). Transfer to a sealed container and cover the top of the sorbet with waxed or greaseproof paper. Transfer to the freezer until needed.

Lime and chocolate sorbet

I wanted to capture the taste of chocolate lime sherbets, and the synthetic sweetness I recall loving as a child (okay, I still love them). The liminess is achieved by the addition of fresh lemon juice, which seems to bring the limes alive.

SERVES 9 single scoops (approx. 700 g)

175 ml stock syrup
1 tbsp glucose syrup (optional)
200 g plain chocolate (min. cocoa solids 70 per cent)
juice of 5 limes
2 tbsp fresh lemon juice

1 Heat the stock syrup in a pan with the glucose syrup, if using.

2 Break up the chocolate into pieces and put in a bowl set over a pan of simmering water. Once the chocolate has melted, pour the warmed stock syrup over it and stir until thoroughly combined.

3 Add 400 ml of water, the lime juice and the lemon juice – the trick is to get the limes to be the dominant flavour set against the secondary richness of the chocolate. Transfer to a covered container and put in the fridge for a couple of hours for the flavours to develop.

4 Churn in an ice-cream machine until firm or follow the still-freezing method (see page 43). Put in a sealed container and cover the top of the sorbet with waxed or greaseproof paper. Transfer to the freezer until needed.

Cats' tongues

Also known in French as 'langues de chat', these finger biscuits, with their hint of lemon, are simple to make and a lovely accompaniment to the two sorbets.

100 g unsalted butter
3 egg whites
100 g caster sugar
2 drops vanilla extract
100 g plain flour, sifted
zest of two unwaxed lemons

1 Pre-heat the oven to 200°C. Allow the butter to soften and the egg whites to come to room temperature before you prepare the recipe.

2 Combine the egg whites and sugar in a bowl on top of a pan of simmering water and warm, stirring occasionally, for a few minutes.

3 In a separate bowl, beat the butter until it is creamy. Stir in the vanilla extract. Add the warmed egg-sugar mixture, a little at a time, and combine, then add the sifted flour and gently beat the mixture till it is smooth.

4 Line a baking tray with non-stick baking paper. Pour the batter into a pastry bag fitted with a 6 mm nozzle. Squeeze the batter out into approximately 20 long finger shapes, leaving lots of space between each one, as the batter tends to spread out; your fingers will end up looking 'webbed' if you don't!

5 Bake in the oven for 10 minutes. The cats' tongues should be a nice amber colour around the edges but slightly soft in the middle.

TO SERVE COUPE CITRON *Allow the sorbets to soften a little. Place a scoop of each sorbet in a coupe glass or dish, placing two cats' tongues alongside the sorbets.*

bombe florentine serves 12

Almond and honey ice cream · Dark chocolate sorbet · Candied orange peel · Candied cherries

A bombe is a frozen dessert of different flavours layered in a mould. I have always loved Florentine biscuits and the way the flavours work together, so I thought it might be fun to make a layered frozen dessert around this concept. This is, therefore, a reconstructed, deconstructed Florentine, so to speak. There are lots of different moulds available, but the easiest ones to use are plastic moulds; you could even use the mould from your Christmas pudding, if you still have it. Moulds come in different shapes as well. If you wanted to be clever, you could use a square mould, line it with ice cream or sorbet at the bottom and around the sides, and then fill the remaining space with your chosen flavour. For this recipe, I have simply created two layers of ice cream and sorbet and added toppings.

A mould size of 16 cm diameter will serve approximately 12.

Almond and honey ice cream

SERVES 8 single scoops (approx. 600 g)

350 ml whole milk
175 ml whipping cream
150 g ground almonds (if you can buy whole blanched almonds and grind them yourself in a coffee grinder, all the better)
4 egg yolks
150 g honey

1 Heat the milk and cream in a pan with the almonds to just below boiling point. Take off the heat and allow the mixture to infuse for 15 minutes, after which strain twice through a chinois or regular sieve.

2 Whisk the egg yolks. Return the strained milk-almond mixture to the pan and reheat. Add the milk to the whisked eggs then return the mixture to the pan again. Heat, stirring continuously, to 80°C on a probe thermometer and maintain for 15 seconds. Do not allow the mix to boil or it will scramble.

3 Take off the heat and continue whisking the mix for a few minutes to reduce the heat. Add the honey and stir it in until thoroughly incorporated. Transfer the mix to a container, and place in an ice bath, in order to cool the custard as quickly as possible to 4°C. Once cooled, cover the container and transfer to the fridge to mature for a minimum of 4 hours (or ideally overnight).

4 Churn in an ice-cream machine till firm or follow the still-freezing method (see page 43). Put in a sealed container and cover the top of the ice cream with waxed or greaseproof paper. Transfer to the freezer until needed.

Dark chocolate sorbet

SERVES 7–8 single scoops (approx. 500 g)

200 ml stock syrup
1 tbsp glucose syrup (optional)
200 g plain chocolate (min. cocoa solids 70 per cent)
1 tbsp cocoa powder
25 ml vodka (optional)

1 Heat the stock syrup and, if using, add the glucose syrup.

2 Break up the chocolate into pieces and put it in a bowl with the cocoa powder. Gradually pour in the stock syrup. Stir for a few minutes to make sure the chocolate and cocoa powder have melted completely. If the cocoa powder is not incorporated properly, the sorbet will have a bitter flavour. Add the vodka, if using, and 150 ml of water and allow the mix to cool.

3 Strain then churn in an ice-cream machine until firm or follow the still-freezing method (see page 43). Put in a sealed container and cover the top of the sorbet with waxed or greaseproof paper. Transfer to the freezer till needed.

Candied orange peel

2 oranges, unwaxed
400 g caster sugar, plus more for tossing

1 Wash the oranges, cut them in half lengthways and squeeze out the juice (you might want to use the juice for some other purpose).

2 Fill a pan with cold water and add the orange halves. Bring to the boil, then reduce the heat and simmer for approximately 10 minutes. Drain the oranges and return them to the pan. Fill the pan again with cold water and repeat this blanching process two more times.

3 Let the oranges rest until they are cool enough to handle then cut the halves in half again and remove any remaining pulp and as much of the white pith as possible, using a teaspoon. Cut the peel into long, thin strips.

4 Bring 200 ml of water and the caster sugar to the boil in a pan. Reduce the heat, add the orange peel and continue to cook gently until the syrup becomes translucent and the bubbles are very small (about 25–30 minutes). If you are using a sugar thermometer, it should reach 110°C. Turn off the heat and let the peel cool in the syrup.

5 Once cool, lift out the peel with a fork, and put it on non-stick baking paper, ensuring the pieces don't touch each other. Leave them for 3–4 hours and then toss the peel in caster sugar.

Candied cherries

250 g cherries, stems removed, stoned
150 g caster sugar

1 Bring 250 ml of water and the sugar to the boil in a pan, then reduce the heat, add the cherries, and simmer on a very low heat, uncovered for about 45 minutes. Don't allow the syrup to boil once the cherries have been added or you will find yourself with a jam!

2 Once the cherries have finished cooking, leave them to cool in the syrup.

3 Strain the cherries (reserving the syrup for something else). Put the cherries on a piece of non-stick baking paper, ensuring they don't touch each other and let them dry (preferably overnight).

4 The candied cherries will keep in a sealed container in the fridge for up to 2 weeks.

TO PREPARE BOMBE FLORENTINE *Place the mould in the freezer for about 30 minutes before it is needed. Remove the Chocolate Sorbet from the freezer about 30 minutes before it is needed, so that it softens to the right consistency. Spoon approximately 500 g of the sorbet into the mould in an even layer. Cover and put in the freezer for an hour.*

Remove the Almond and Honey Ice Cream from the freezer about 30 minutes before it is needed and allow it to soften. Take the mould out of the freezer and spoon approximately 500 g of the ice cream into the mould in an even layer (or as much as it takes to fill the mould to the base). Cover and return to the freezer for a couple of hours or until needed.

TO SERVE BOMBE FLORENTINE *Remove the filled mould from the freezer and put it in the fridge for 30–45 minutes so that it softens evenly. Check it by inserting a knife into the centre; if the knife goes in easily, the bombe is ready. If it feels too soft, place it back into the freezer. If it still feels too hard, leave it at room temperature for a while, but check it carefully.*

Fill a large bowl with lukewarm water, and insert the mould in the water for about 10 seconds, making sure the water does not come over the edge.

Turn the mould onto a platter – the bombe should slide out easily. Cover and return the bombe to the freezer for 30 minutes for the sides to harden again. Do the knife test again, and, when ready, top the bombe with the candied cherries and orange peel and 50 g of sliced almonds.

coupe concorde serves 8

Dark chocolate ice cream · Orange ice cream · Orange confit

Coupe Concorde is normally made with chocolate ice cream topped with a custard-based orange sauce – I have merely changed the sauce into an ice cream. I serve this with an orange confit and lady's finger biscuits (which I buy), so that when everything is eaten together, it tastes just like a gooey Jaffa cake.

Dark Chocolate Ice Cream (see page 56)

Orange ice cream

SERVES 8 single scoops (approx. 600 g)

3 large oranges (preferably unwaxed)
250 ml whole milk
250 ml whipping cream
3 egg yolks
125 g caster sugar
 or 110 g caster sugar and 1 tbsp glucose syrup

1 Wash the oranges and dry them. Remove the zest from the oranges with a vegetable peeler. Put the zest into a pan with the milk, the cream and the glucose syrup, if using, and bring to just below boiling point. Turn off the heat and allow the zest to infuse for 15 minutes. Strain and discard the zest. Juice the oranges.

2 Beat the egg yolks with the sugar. Reheat the milk and add it to the egg-sugar mix then return the mixture to the pan. Heat, stirring continuously, to 80°C on a probe thermometer and maintain for 15 seconds. Do not allow the mix to boil or it will scramble.

3 Remove the custard from the heat and continue whisking for a few minutes to reduce the heat, then transfer the mix to a container, and place in an ice bath, in order to cool the custard as quickly as possible to 4°C. Add the orange juice then put in a covered container and place in the fridge to mature for a minimum of 4 hours (or ideally overnight).

4 Churn in an ice-cream machine until firm or follow the still-freezing method (see page 43). Put in a sealed container and cover the top of the ice cream with waxed or greaseproof paper. Transfer to the freezer until needed.

Orange confit

4 large oranges (approx. 160 ml juice)
100 g caster sugar
100 g glucose syrup
16 lady's fingers

1 Wash the oranges, remove the peel with a vegetable peeler and cut it into fine strips. Remove any leftover white pith then cut the oranges in half lengthways and squeeze out the juice, reserving for later. Put the zest into a pan, cover with water then bring to the boil and simmer for 10 minutes in order to blanch it. Drain.

2 Put the sugar, glucose syrup, orange juice, zest and 100 ml of water into a pan and slowly bring to the boil. Turn down the heat and simmer for an hour, then allow the confit to cool. Set aside until needed.

TO SERVE COUPE CONCORDE *Allow the ice creams to soften a little. Put two lady's finger biscuits into a bowl. Place a scoop of each ice cream on top. Spoon the Orange confit onto the ice creams.*

coupe aromatique

serves 8–9

Lemon verbena and rose petal ice cream · Scented geranium ice cream · Candied rose petals

I love the way this floral-based sundae evokes the exotic and sumptuous flavours of Turkish Delight.

Lemon verbena and rose petal ice cream

The flavours that come through here conjure up the heady aromatics of an English garden. The recipe includes the optional use of mastic, a resin from the mastic tree that is used as a thickening gum in Turkish delight. It can be found for sale in Middle Eastern shops, where it is sold in small packets for chewing as a gum. It is by no means necessary to include it in the recipe, but it does give the ice cream a slightly elastic texture similar to the Middle Eastern ice cream Dondurma Kaymakli. *Please note you should only use unsprayed rose petals for this recipe.*

SERVES 8–9 single scoops (approx. 650 g)

500 ml whole milk
100 ml whipping cream
150 g caster sugar
    or 135 g caster sugar and 1 tbsp glucose syrup
1/8 tsp mastic (optional)
approx. 20 unsprayed rose petals
approx. 10 lemon verbena leaves
3 egg yolks

1 Heat the milk, cream, half the sugar and glucose syrup, if using, in a pan to just below boiling point. If you are using mastic, crush and pulverise the mastic by pounding it with a little extra caster sugar, and stir it into the milk until it dissolves.

2 Add the rose petals and lemon verbena leaves, and turn off the heat. Allow them to infuse for 15 minutes (some roses are more aromatic than others so taste after 15 minutes to check).

3 Strain the milk and discard the rose petals and lemon verbena. Whisk the egg yolks with the remaining sugar. Add the strained warm milk to the egg–sugar mix and return the mixture to the pan. Heat the custard, stirring continuously, to 80°C on a probe thermometer and maintain for 15 seconds. Do not allow the mix to boil or it will scramble.

4 Turn off the heat and continue whisking the custard for a few minutes to reduce the heat. Ttransfer the mix to a container, and place in an ice bath, in order to cool the custard as quickly as possible to 4°C. Put the custard in a sealed container in the fridge to mature for a minimum of 4 hours (or ideally overnight).

5 Churn in an ice-cream machine until firm or follow the still-freezing method (see page 43). Put in a sealed container and cover the top of the ice cream with waxed or greaseproof paper. Transfer to the freezer until needed.

Scented geranium ice cream

Scented geraniums, or pelargoniums, have different scents according to their type, including aromas of rose, nutmeg, lemon and mint. The flower flavour generally corresponds to the variety; so lemon-scented geraniums have, naturally, lemon-scented flowers and so on.

SERVES 8–9 single scoops (approx. 650 g)

500 ml whole milk
100 ml whipping cream
150 g caster sugar
   or 135 g caster sugar and 1 tbsp glucose syrup
5 geranium flowers
3 egg yolks

1 Heat the milk, cream, half the sugar and glucose syrup, if using, in a pan to just below boiling point.

2 Wash and dry the flower heads and add these to the warmed milk. Turn off the heat and allow them to infuse for 15 minutes. Strain the milk and discard the geranium flowers.

3 Whisk the egg yolks with the remaining sugar. Add the warm strained milk to the egg-sugar mix and return the mixture to the pan. Heat the custard, stirring continuously, to 80°C on a probe thermometer and maintain for 15 seconds. Do not allow the mix to boil or it will scramble.

4 Turn off the heat and continue whisking the custard for a few minutes to reduce the heat. Transfer it to a container that can be placed on an ice bath to cool the custard as rapidly as possible to 4°C. Put the custard in a sealed container in the fridge to mature for a minimum of 4 hours or overnight.

5 Churn in an ice-cream machine until firm or follow the still-freezing method (see page 43). Put in a sealed container and cover the top of the ice cream with waxed or greaseproof paper. Transfer to the freezer until needed.

Candied rose petals

This recipe contains raw egg white.

3 egg whites
24–27 unsprayed rose petals
100 g caster sugar

1 Whisk the egg whites. Wash and pat dry the rose petals then dip them in the egg whites and then in the sugar.

2 Put the rose petals on waxed or greaseproof paper to dry, preferably overnight. Store in an airtight container until needed.

TO SERVE COUPE AROMATIQUE *Allow the ice creams to soften a little. Put a scoop of each ice cream in a glass bowl and scatter 2–3 rose petals per person over each scoop.*

coupe cardinal serves 12

Vanilla ice cream · Blackcurrant sorbet · Blackcurrant sauce

This is a classic sundae where the addition of a sauce that matches the flavour of the sorbet intensifies the overall taste experience.

Vanilla Ice Cream (see page 53)

Blackcurrant sorbet

SERVES 12 single scoops (approx. 900 g)

1 kg blackcurrants
1 tbsp glucose syrup (optional)
200 ml stock syrup

1 Bring about 1 1/2 litres of water to the boil in a large pan. Add the blackcurrants to the boiling water and stir for a few minutes over a high heat until the water comes back to the boil. Drain and cool.

2 Mash the blackcurrants through a sieve to extract as much pulp and juice as possible. Discard the remaining stalks and skins.

3 If using glucose syrup, combine with the stock syrup and heat in a pan until the glucose syrup dissolves. Allow to cool.

4 Combine the stock syrup with the fruit purée. Churn in an ice-cream machine until firm or follow the still-freezing method (see page 43). Put into a sealed container and cover the top of the sorbet with waxed or greaseproof paper. Transfer to the freezer until needed.

Blackcurrant sauce

500 g blackcurrants
50 ml stock syrup

1 Bring about 1 litre of water to the boil in a large pan. Add the blackcurrants to the boiling water and stir for a few minutes over a high heat until the water comes back to the boil. Drain and cool.

2 Mash the blackcurrants through a sieve to extract as much pulp and juice as possible. Discard the remaining stalks and skins.

3 Combine the stock syrup with the fruit purée. Set aside until needed.

TO SERVE COUPE CARDINAL *Allow the Vanilla Ice Cream and the Blackcurrant Sorbet to soften a little. Place a scoop of each in a coupe dish or glass. Top with the Blackcurrant Sauce and some extra blackcurrants on top, for decoration.*

black forest sundae serves 12

Chocolate brownies · Cherry sorbet · Morello cherry compote ·
Crème chantilly

Another deconstruction, this time of Black Forest gateau. I have been serving
this sundae from my ice-cream van from the outset, and of course, since
Black Forest gateau is such a favourite classic, so is this.

Chocolate Brownies (see page 67)

Cherry sorbet

SERVES 12–13 single scoops (approx. 1 kg)

1 tbsp glucose syrup (optional)
200 ml stock syrup
1.3 kg fresh cherries
juice of 1 lime

1 If you are using glucose syrup, combine with the stock syrup and heat in a pan
until the syrup is dissolved.

2 De-stem and pit the cherries. Put them in a blender and blend to a purée.
Strain– you will have approximately 800 g of purée.

3 Combine the purée with the stock syrup and lime juice. Churn in an ice-cream
machine until firm or follow the still-freezing method (see page 43). Put in a sealed
container and cover the top of the sorbet with waxed or greaseproof paper.
Transfer to the freezer until needed.

Morello cherry compote

If you cannot find fresh morello (sour) cherries in the markets (and they are hard
to find), you can either replace them with the sweet cherries that are readily
available in the summer or else use bottled morello cherries. In this event, I would
always choose the latter option, because sweet cherries just do not have the

intensity of flavour of sour cherries, nor do they work as well with the kirsch-flavoured sugar syrup. If you go for the bottled-cherries option, discard the syrup and make your own.

The cherry compote will keep for up to 2 weeks if stored in a sealed container in the fridge.

300 g morello cherries or 350 g bottled morello cherries
  (approx. 200 g after straining the syrup)
275 g caster sugar
1 tsp fresh lemon juice
50 ml kirsch

1 If using fresh cherries, remove the stems and pit the cherries.

2 Bring 275 ml of water, the caster sugar and lemon juice to the boil in a pan, reduce the heat and add the cherries. Simmer for 15 minutes.

3 Strain the cherries and return the syrup to the pan. Reduce the syrup by half.

4 Add the kirsch. Allow to cool. Combine the cherry syrup with the cherries. Serve hot or cold.

5 If using bottled cherries, strain the cherries and discard the syrup.

6 Bring 275 ml of water, the caster sugar and lemon juice to the boil in a pan, reduce the heat and simmer for 25-30 minutes.

7 Add the kirsch. Allow to cool. Add the cherries. Serve hot or cold.

Crème chantilly

300 ml whipping cream
25 g caster sugar
grated plain chocolate, to serve

1 Combine the cream with the sugar in a mixing bowl and beat until the cream has doubled in volume and forms soft peaks.

2 Cover and place in the fridge until needed.

TO SERVE BLACK FOREST SUNDAE *Allow the Cherry Sorbet to soften a little. Put a slice of Chocolate Brownie on a plate and spoon the Morello Cherry Compote alongside. Top the brownie with a scoop of sorbet and a generous serving of Crème Chantilly. Top with the grated chocolate.*

vacherin aux marrons serves 8

Chestnut ice cream · Meringue · Crème chantilly

This sundae is simple to make but looks fabulous. It is essentially a big ice cream 'sandwich' – chestnut ice cream encased in two meringue discs topped with a big dollop of cream. Yummy!

Chestnut ice cream

SERVES 7–8 single scoops (approx. 1.1 kg)

240 g whole cooked and peeled chestnuts
300 ml whipping cream
200 g caster sugar
500 ml whole milk
5 egg yolks
2 tbsp dark rum
1/2 tsp vanilla extract

1 Put the chestnuts and half the whipping cream in a blender and purée.

2 Heat the milk and the remaining cream in a pan to just below boiling point. Whisk the egg yolks with the sugar. Add the warm milk to the egg–sugar mix and return the mixture to the pan. Heat, stirring continuously, to 80°C on a probe thermometer and maintain for 15 seconds. Do not allow the mix to boil or it will scramble.

3 Take the custard off the heat and continue whisking for a few minutes to reduce the heat. Transfer the mix to a container, and place in an ice bath, to cool the custard as quickly as possible to 4°C. Fold in the chestnut purée, rum and vanilla extract.

4 Once cooled, strain the custard. Put the custard in a sealed container in the fridge to mature for a minimum of 4 hours (or ideally overnight).

5 Churn in an ice-cream machine until firm or follow the still-freezing method (see page 43). Put in a sealed container and cover the top of the ice cream with waxed or greaseproof paper. Transfer to the freezer until needed.

Meringue

SERVES 8

250 g caster sugar
6 egg whites
250 g ground almonds
10 g unsalted butter, for buttering

1 Pre-heat the oven to 150°C. Cut two circles, approximately 22 cm in diameter, from two pieces of greaseproof or non-stick baking paper. Grease the papers and put on two baking trays.

2 Put some water into a small pan and bring it to the boil, then reduce to a simmer. Put the sugar and egg whites into a bowl and set it over the pan of simmering water, then stir until the sugar dissolves. The mixture should be quite warm.

3 Whisk the mixture, preferably with an electric mixer, until it is thick and glossy. Fold in the ground almonds.

4 Spoon the meringue onto the non-stick baking paper within the circles. Put the baking sheets in the oven, then turn off the oven and leave the meringues to dry out overnight.

Crème chantilly (see page 229)

TO SERVE VACHERIN AUX MARRONS *Allow the Chestnut Ice Cream to soften a little. Spoon the Chestnut Ice Cream over one meringue disc. Cover with the second disc. Top the second disc with the Crème Chantilly. Grate dark chocolate over the Crème Chantilly. Serve with aplomb!*

5 Equipment

You will need...

This list of equipment is by no means exhaustive, but it does include everything necessary for domestic ice-cream and sorbet making.

Blender It is worth buying a full sized blender as opposed to a hand-held one as you will enable you to make smooth purées of uniform consistency without any fuss.

Chinois A chinois is a conical strainer that holds more liquid than a regular strainer and fits neatly onto a measuring jug – meaning you can strain liquids and purées more easily. They can be purchased from cookware or catering shops.

Cocktail sticks These are useful as skewers for fruit that can then be stuck into the top of an ice cream. Kebab skewers are good for heavier fruit.

Coffee grinder These useful little things not only grind fresh coffee beans but also grind nuts. Make sure the grinder is free of any coffee debris before you put nuts into it, however! If a recipe calls for ground nuts, buy the whole blanched nuts and grind them yourself – they will have a much fresher flavour.

Containers If you can buy small, square metal containers from a catering shop, do so. They are perfect for cooling custard in. Metal transfers heat faster than other materials, so, theoretically, your custard should cool quicker if placed in a metal container. That said, I have compared metal and plastic containers side by side and in all honesty the custard in the metal container did not cool that much quicker than that in the plastic one. Nevertheless, they are rather useful things to have at hand for cooling custards.

Espresso maker A small Italian stove-top espresso maker is cheap and makes good, strong coffee – ideal for making an espresso granita, for example.

Freezer packs I use these in lieu of ice cubes when chilling custard as quickly as possible. Keep 3–4 of them in your freezer.

Fridge and freezer thermometers It is always useful to know your fridge and freezer temperatures, so that you can adjust them accordingly.

Grater For grating lemon, lime and orange zest without removing the white pith.

Ice-cream machines Not mandatory, but ice cream and sorbet making is a great deal easier if you have one since they incorporate air into the ice cream or sorbet. This is much harder to achieve using the still-freezing method. There are various types of ice-cream machine available on the market:

Pre-frozen canister machines These are rather clever and not very expensive. A liquid coolant in a sealed jacket surrounds the canister. If placed in the freezer, the coolant will freeze much like a freezer pack, but it needs to be left in the freezer overnight in order to cool sufficiently; it is then put back into the machine, and the dasher, or paddle, is inserted before the mix is added and churned. If you don't leave the canister in the freezer for long enough, the mix won't freeze, so it is important not to veer from the manufacturer's instructions.

There is a wide range of these available on the market, and they are perfect for the occasional ice-cream maker. It is worth purchasing two canisters and keeping them both in the freezer. This will mean you do not need to plan too far in advance if you decide to make an ice cream or sorbet; also that you can make more than one batch without having to wait for the canister to re-freeze.

Self-refrigerating machines These machines have a built-in compressor and, although much more expensive, are a worthwhile purchase for anyone who is keen on making ice creams and sorbets on a regular basis. They do not require any advanced planning, such as ensuring you have chilled canisters, and one batch after another of freshly churned ice cream or sorbet can be made.

Pacojet A rather interesting way of making ice cream and sorbet. Instead of churning your pre-prepared custard or sorbet mix in the normal way, you freeze it in a canister. When it is completely frozen, you attach the canister to the machine, and a razor-sharp blade 'shaves' the mix into a perfectly smooth textured product within a few minutes. It is not only ice cream and sorbet that can be made using a Pacojet but whatever other foods you might wish to freeze as well, such as soup. Sorbets can also be made without adding any sugar to them.

I love my Pacojet but buying it did leave a big dent in my bank balance. I also have to adapt some of my recipes if I am making ice cream with a Pacojet rather than a self-refrigerating machine, so I like to have both. One of the advantages of using a Pacojet is that you can make batches of ice cream and sorbet, freeze them, and then only 'shave' the quantity that you need for a particular occasion.

Ice-cube tray You can cool custard over an ice bath using water and ice cubes or freezer packs. Ice-cube trays have another purpose: a cheat's way of making sorbet. Purée fruit and put it into an ice-cube tray and freeze. Then blitz the ice cubes in a blender or food processor – you will have made sorbet.

Juicer For making fresh juices to add to ice creams, such as Burnt Orange Caramel Ice Cream (see page 88), or for juicing vegetables.

Knives A good-quality, sharp knife is indispensable for chopping fruit and vegetables. A 20 cm chef's knife will do the job and also a small, 10 cm paring knife is good for removing stones from fruit.

Liquidiser See Blender.

Loaf tin A loaf tin or terrine mould of approximately 23 x 10.5 x 6 cm is useful for freezing ice cream or sorbet in a terrine shape, or for baking chocolate brownies.

Mandolin The inexpensive plastic ones are perfect for slicing fruit into very thin slices so that they can be candied.

Measuring jugs Required for reasons too obvious to mention. It is useful to have a few of them around, especially plastic ones, which are durable.

Mixer An electric hand-mixer will do if you do not wish to flex your muscles with a manual whisk.

Mixing bowls Any type of bowl will do – plastic, glass or stainless steel. It is always worth having a few large bowls around for tempering egg yolks or pouring your custard into.

Moulds Moulds specially designed for ice creams and sorbet are made of metal and come with a lid. However, I find it just as easy to use a plastic mould (even if it has no lid) or even use the mould from my Christmas pudding. Plastic moulds are more flexible than metal ones, making it easier to pry out a recalcitrant bombe.

Savarin moulds of 10 cm are useful for making Rum Baba (see page 206). It is also useful to have dariole moulds at hand for kulfis (see page 145) or if you fancy making a chocolate pot or chocolate fondant to go with your ice cream.

Non-stick baking paper or waxed paper This protects the ice cream or sorbet from shrinkage once it has been placed in the freezer for storage.

Oven thermometer In-built oven thermometers are not always very accurate, so it is useful to keep a small stand-alone thermometer in the oven for double-checking the temperature.

Pans Heavy-duty pans are best as they ensure an even distribution of heat when custard is being cooked. Use non-reactive pans (of anodised aluminium or lined with stainless steel) if heating fruit-based mixtures or anything, like wine, that is acidic.

Pestle and mortar I'm a bit of an old-fashioned girl – I like to grind my spices with a pestle and mortar. They are so inexpensive and look lovely, and they get the best out of your spices.

Probe thermometer Another mandatory piece of equipment if you are concerned about pasteurising your custard. A digital thermometer is very accurate, although when taking a reading from it, ensure that the probe is submerged in the custard, not touching the bottom of the pan, which is hotter than the custard itself.

Scales Mandatory for weighing ingredients. Both balance and digital scales are fine.

Scoops You can either purchase a spring-loaded scoop, which has a piece of metal that releases the ice cream into a perfectly formed ball, or a simple scoop, which comes in various sizes according to how many scoops can be served from a litre of ice cream. I prefer the latter.

Sieves Necessary for straining liquids, purées and custards. Small sieves are useful for straining lemon juice; large sieves for removing pips and fibres from purées.

Spatula Flexible rubber or plastic spatulas made from heatproof material are pretty handy for stirring custard.

Storage boxes I prefer to store my ices in plastic containers with tight-fitting lids. It is better if they are not too large as ices are best stored in a few small containers than one large one (if you are only using a little at a time, this prevents subjecting the remaining ice cream or sorbet to too many temperature fluctuations). If you own a Pacojet, this comes with stainless-steel containers.

Sundae dishes These come in various forms, usually made of glass. They can be found in good kitchen or catering shops and always make ice creams look extra special.

Vegetable peeler This can be used to remove zest from citrus fruit or for peeling fruit like mangoes.

Whisks I use a whisk or a spatula to stir custard as it is cooking. Whisks are also handy if you wish to whip your egg yolks by hand.

6 Questions & Answers

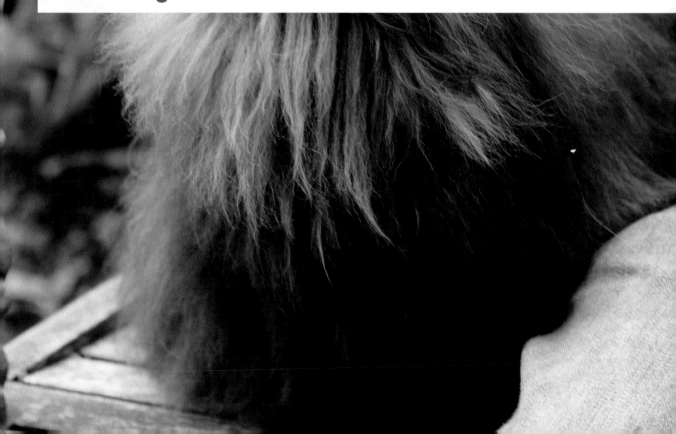

Your ice-cream dilemmas solved

Q Can ice cream be made without cooking any of the ingredients?

A Yes. You can combine cream and/or milk with a flavouring and sugar then blend them together and churn the mix in an ice-cream machine or by the still-freezing method, and you will have made ice cream. It is called Philadelphia-style ice cream because dairy farming was widespread in the state of Philadelphia and much of the excess produce was channelled into ice-cream production. The ice cream was always 'uncooked' and contained simply cream, sugar and vanilla. 'Philadelphia-style' ice cream now refers to any ice cream made without a custard base.

Q How long should a flavour be allowed to infuse for?

A The period for which an ingredient should infuse is dependent upon the product itself, and whether it is fresh or dried. For example, a dried vanilla pod or cinnamon stick will take longer to impart its flavour than freshly grated lemon zest. Bear in mind that a custard base with a high fat content (especially if you add double cream) will mute the flavours of anything infused, so make sure that the initial infusion is strong. As a general rule, 15 minutes is the minimum time needed for flavour to be extracted and you are unlikely to get any further extraction if you leave an ingredient to infuse for over an hour. The best test is to taste everything as you go along.

Q Do you need to re-pasteurise eggs and dairy products?

A Even if both your eggs and your dairy products have already been pasteurised, it is generally safer to re-pasteurise to the required temperature. Although you may get some denaturation of the whey proteins above 65°C, it is not significant unless the custard is subjected to excessive heat treatment (say, 85–90°C for 25 seconds or longer)

Q Is there anything I can do to prevent my custard from scrambling?

A If you add a pinch of flour to the custard before you start to cook it, this will prevent any possibility of the custard scrambling, as, at high enough temperatures, the molecules of flour pass into solution and block the aggregation of the egg's proteins. It will mean that those with gluten allergies cannot eat the ice cream.

If you do find yourself with custard that has partially scrambled, this can be retrieved by putting the custard in a bowl in a sink full of cold water and whisking as rapidly as possible. Do this if there is only a small amount scrambled – if the whole thing looks like scrambled eggs, chuck it away and start again!

Q How can I cool my custard as quickly as possible?

A Getting your custard to cool rapidly is pretty difficult in a home kitchen and there is no real way that you can tell whether it has reached 4°C without using a probe thermometer. (It may feel cold enough when you dip your finger in the custard but it may not necessarily be so.) One way to speed up the cooling process is by cooling it down to about 20°C by using an ice bath, then covering the container and putting it in the freezer to cool it further to the required temperature. You must keep an eye on it though to ensure it does not freeze!

Another way to speed up the cooling process only applies to ice creams that have a fruit or vegetable purée added to them, such as strawberry ice cream. This method requires a little advanced planning – the fruit or vegetable should be puréed the day before you intend to make the custard, and then frozen. Once you have made the custard and are cooling it, add the frozen purée. This will lower the temperature of the custard immediately.

Q Should an ice-cream mix without eggs still be cooled as rapidly as possible?

A Yes, ideally, the milk–cream mix should still be cooled as quickly as possible to prevent any bacteria being allowed to develop.

Q What is the difference, if any, between ice cream and gelato?

A Italian ice cream or gelato (which simply means 'frozen') often contains little or no cream (though this does vary regionally) and uses milk and eggs as its primary building blocks. Because milk has less fat in it than cream, it is not able to form a fat membrane in which to hold the air that is churned into it in the same way as an ice cream with a greater percentage of cream. There is, therefore, less air incorporated into a traditional gelato, and this makes it denser. Paradoxically, gelatos tend to seem richer than ice creams, even though they have less fat in them, and are often perceived as being more flavour intense than ice creams. This is because a product with a lower fat content diffuses the perception of flavour quicker to the taste receptors than a creamier ice cream where cream coats the tongue with melting fat droplets, slowing down the transfer and perception of flavour to the taste receptors.

The food writer David Lebovitz says in his book on ice cream, *The Perfect Scoop*, that although some gelatos do have egg yolks, they are often thickened with a starch instead, which results in a gelato that tastes less rich than a custard-based one. He also adds that the freezers used to hold gelato in Italy are kept at a higher temperature, −12°C, in order to keep it soft, as opposed to the regular freezers that are set at approximately −19°C.

Q Should stabilisers be used in ice cream?

A If an ice cream is consumed within a few days of making it, it will not have the opportunity to have its structure altered by changes in the size, shape and quantity of its ice crystals. Since ice crystals within ice creams are unstable, the longer an ice cream is stored in a freezer (or subject to 'heat shock' – that is the effects of bringing an ice cream out of the freezer and up to serving temperature and then lowering its temperature again once it is returned to the freezer), the greater the danger of ice re-crystallisation. Also known as Ostwald ripening, in this process the water in the ice cream re-crystallises, with larger ice crystals growing at the expense of smaller ones. The ice cream becomes increasingly 'coarse' or 'icy'. Stabilisers prevent or inhibit this, as they adsorb to the ice crystal surfaces, literally binding the frozen water to them. Stabilisers may also prevent lactose crystal growth.

Stabilisers are primarily natural products and include locust bean gum, Guar Guar, Sodium alginate, Carrageenan, an extract of Irish moss or other red algae, and gelatine. Some cooks add marshmallows to their ice cream to stabilise it, though these ices cannot be eaten by vegetarians.

I do not add stabilisers to my ice creams because I do not keep them for longer than a week and therefore there is little danger of ice re-crystalisation.

Some cooks also opt for the alternative so-called 'French' method of preventing coarsening of their ice creams and sorbets by simply allowing them to melt down (but not de-frost) partially and then re-churning them for a smooth texture.

Q What is invert sugar and what is its role in ice-cream making?

A Sucrose is a disaccharide made up of one molecule of glucose (also known as dextrose) and one molecule of fructose (also known as levulose), chemically bonded together. If sucrose is broken down into its component parts, the process is known as 'inversion'. Invert sugar syrups can be fully inverted into equal quantities of fructose and glucose, or partially inverted to leave part of the original sucrose unchanged. Sucrose can easily be inverted by the use of an acid (such as lemon juice or cream of tartar), heat and water, and that makes the mixture sweeter. Fructose is twice as sweet as sucrose, but glucose is only about three quarters of the sweetness of sucrose, so fully inverted sugar is approximately 37 per cent sweeter than sucrose. All invert sugars exist only as a syrup, as fructose won't crystallise in the presence of glucose and sucrose.

While invert sugar sounds somewhat mysterious and complicated, it is actually present in a variety of our daily products. When jam is made, combining the sugar with the acid in the fruit and heating it automatically creates invert sugar. Honey is primarily an invert sugar as bees have an enzyme called invertase that inverts the sugar collected from pollen and converts the sugars within it into fructose and dextrose. Every bottle of champagne or sparkling wine that is produced by the traditional method contains sucrose that has been inverted by the acids within the wine into equal parts of glucose and fructose.

Invert sugar has its benefits in ice-cream making as it improves the texture of an ice cream by making it softer as the sucrose crystals have been split into their smaller, finer monosaccharides. They have a lower molecular weight than disaccharides and twice the freezing point depression so the mix will take longer to freeze and more air has a chance to be incorporated into it, making the ice cream softer. The use of invert sugar in your ice cream will also make it lower in calories as less of it is needed to achieve the desired sweetness. However you would be adding additional water to the mix, which would alter its composition, in which case you would need to substitute some of the whole milk with skimmed milk in order to maintain the water ratio and suddenly it all feels quite complicated! In addition, although you may make a softer, lower calorie ice cream, its shelf life will be reduced because it is more prone to re-crystallisation since there is a greater unfrozen 'phase' at any given temperature. In other words, it won't keep!

The stock syrup in this recipe book is partially inverted because it contains lemon juice. The level of inversion is low as it is brought to the boil and simmered for only a brief period and therefore not fully inverted. The purpose of adding the enzyme to the syrup is to stabilise it – stock syrups have a tendency to partially crystallise back to a solid if some of the water has boiled away and the solution is saturated with sucrose. Introducing another type of sugar, such as fructose or glucose, into the composition, will slow down the level of re-crystallisation, as the fructose and glucose molecules will get in the way of the sucrose molecules (because they are a different size and shape), stopping them from locking together to form crystals. By inverting the stock syrup with the addition of an acid or enzyme, fructose and glucose are introduced, and this will prevent crystallisation of the syrup. Alternatively, if glucose syrup is added to the stock syrup, this will have the same effect. (If you were to make candies, the principle is the same – introduce other type of sugars, such as fructose, glucose or glucose syrup into the mix so that their molecules get in the way of sucrose molecules and prevent them from locking together to form crystals.)

Q Are there different types of glucose syrup?

A Yes. Glucose syrups are defined by their Dextrose Equivalent, known as DE, which is the specification used to describe how much the dextrose (starch) molecule has been broken down into its simpler sugars. If starch is completely hydrolysed into pure glucose units, it will have a DE of 100 as all the bonds from the original starch molecule has been broken. A medium hydrolysis produces a chain of sugars, including glucose, maltose, maltotriose and maltodextrins. A low conversion yields a DE of 30–44 with low levels of glucose, maltose and maltotriose but high levels of maltodextrins. It is this high level of maltodextrin that gives glucose syrup its high viscosity because it ties up more water in the mix thereby supplying a greater stabilising effect against coarse texture.

The glucose syrups most commonly available are those with low levels of conversion into their simpler sugars and it is these that are of most use to the ice cream and sorbet maker. Specialist food companies supply dehydrated glucose, or atomised glucose, which is more water absorbent than liquid glucose.

Q Can you take a sorbet recipe and make a granita out of it, or vice versa?

A Well, yes, you can, but the level of sweetness of a recipe affects the texture of the final product. Since sorbet needs more sugar (or sucrose substitutes) than granita to give body and improve its viscosity, you may not get the result you want. Not only does sugar make a sorbet smoother, it also lowers the freezing point depression during churning. Water freezes out of a solution in its pure form, leaving behind a very concentrated sugar solution that has a continually lowered freezing point with increased concentration. This prevents sorbets from freezing into a solid block of ice and makes them scoopable at subzero temperatures. These factors are not relevant to granita as the whole point of them is to produce as coarse a texture as possible. If you make granita using too much sugar, you won't get a coarse-textured granita, but a sticky mass of crystals, as the sugar prevents proper crystallisation.

Q What is freezing point depression?

A Freezing point depression is the phenomenon that occurs when something is added to a liquid that lowers its freezing point. It occurs at two areas in the ice-cream making process – in the ice-cream mix itself as it is being frozen and in the external cylinder of the ice-cream machine, which contains a solution of brine. To make ice cream with an old-fashioned hand-crank machine, you need ice and rock salt to make the cream mixture cold enough to freeze because the freezing point of salt water is lower than that of pure water. The principles are the same as when you add salt to icy roads since salt lowers the freezing point of water to below 0°C and makes the ice melt. In an ice-cream machine, the temperature of the ice–salt mixture in the outer container can go below the normal freezing point of water making it possible to freeze the ice-cream mixture in the inner container.

At the freezing point, ice and water are in dynamic equilibrium with each other. The tendency of ice to melt is counteracted by the tendency of water to freeze. In other words, nothing happens! Adding a solute to it will disrupt this equilibrium, as the concentration of water in the solution will go down since the solute molecules have replaced the water molecules. There are less water molecules 'captured' by the ice per second and less water molecules to freeze. The added solute slows down the rate of freezing while the rate of melting is unaffected, so melting occurs faster than freezing.

Salt lowers the freezing point of a solution to a greater degree than sugar: 10 g of sodium chloride (salt) added to 100 ml of water will lower the freezing point to −5.9°C whereas 10 g of sucrose added to a 100 g of water will reduce the freezing point down to −0.56°C. Sodium chloride has a lower molecular weight than sucrose and the lower the weight, the greater the ability of a molecule to depress the freezing point. Adding a pinch of salt to an ice cream mix will lower its freezing point, but putting a sugar solution into the external cylinder of an ice cream machine would not be an effective way of lowering the freezing point of an ice cream.

Q Why is my ice cream or sorbet 'crumbly'?

A It could be because it does not have enough total solids, or enough emulsifier or it has been over-churned. Sadly, it is not really possible to tell whether a crumbly ice cream or sorbet is the consequence of a faulty recipe or of over- churning!

Q How long will my ice creams, sorbets, sherbets and granitas keep for?

A Ice creams, sorbets, sherbets and granitas will keep for an indefinite period if stored at a constant, uninterrupted low temperature of below −25°C. Most home freezers are set at around −19°C, low enough to preserve the ice creams and sorbets, but not really low enough to prevent coarse ice crystals from growing over a gradual period; re-crystallisation will definitely take place if the ice cream is subject to fluctuations in temperature by being taken back and forth from the freezer. The question is: would you want to keep it? Apart from the changes in texture, you will also find that there is a gradual loss of flavour, or unpredictable changes in flavour, so it is generally best to consume anything you have made within a week – if you can actually hang on to it that long!

Bibliography

Adrià, Ferran, Juli Soler and Albert Adrià, *El Bulli 1998-2002* (New York, 2005)

Balaguer, Oriol, *Dessert Cuisine* (Barcelona, 2006)

David, Elizabeth, *Spices, Salt and Aromatics in the English Kitchen* (London, 2000)

Davidson, Alan, *The Oxford Companion to Food* (Oxford, 1999)

Goff, H.D., *Ice Cream – Dairy Science and Technology Education* (www. Foodsci.uoguelph.ca/dairyedu/icecream.html, University of Guelph Ontario, Canada)

Grewling, Peter P., *Chocolates and Confections* (London, 2007)

Gyngell, Skye, *A Year in My Kitchen* (London, 2006)

Keller, Thomas, *The French Laundry Cookbook* (Muskogee, 1999)

Koxholt, M.M.R., B. Eisenmann and J. Hinrichs, ' *Effect of the Fat Globule Sizes on the Meltdown of Ice Cream'*, Journal of Dairy Science (84:31-37)

Lebovitz, David, *The Perfect Scoop* (Berkeley, 2007)

Liddell, Caroline and Robin Weir, *Ices: The Definitive Guide* (London, 2003)

Lister, Ted and Heston Blumenthal, *Kitchen Chemistry* (Cambridge, 2005)

Lucas, P.S., *'Common Defects of Ice Cream, Their Causes and Control; A Review'*, Journal of Dairy Science (Vol 24 No 4 339-368)

Mabey, Richard, *The Complete New Herbal* (London, 1991)

McGee, Harold, *McGee on Food and Cooking* (London, 2004)

Phillips, Roger, *Wild Food* (London, 1983)

Prince, Rose, *The Savvy Shopper* (London, 2006)

This, Herve, *Kitchen Mysteries: Revealing the Science of Cooking* (New York, 2007)

Webb, B.H and S.A. Hall, *'Some Physical Effects of Freezing Upon Milk and Cream'*, Journal of Dairy Science (Vol XV111 No 5)

White, Marco Pierre, *White Heat* (Pyramid Books, 1990)

Index

Acknowledgements

I have received enormous support and encouragement during the writing of this book. My very grateful thanks go to Jeremy Day, for his boundless enthusiasm and support during the entire course of this project. My thanks also go to Professor Douglas Goff at the Department of Food Science, University of Geulph, Canada, who was an invaluable source of information on dairy science and who, very helpfully, answered all of my email queries. Thank you also to the numerous members of the food forum egullet, who have been an extremely useful source of information. My thanks also go to Gillian Etherton, for sharing her glorious Wimbledon garden with me – a place that has inspired many of these recipes and the location for these photographs.

My thanks go to my editor, Imogen Fortes, for commissioning this book and for her tireless enthusiasm in whipping it into shape; and to Vanessa Courtier for capturing its spirit so well through her photographs. My thanks also go to my niece Daisy Jacobsen and nephew Johnny Jacobsen for modelling for this book. To my dearest friend Nick Tarayan, who took me to El Bulli and who would have loved to have seen the story of Mr. Frosty in print. My very special thanks go to the fabulous Rosey Hurst and to the following very special friends who tasted, discussed, inspired and cajoled me and who didn't mind me droning on about freezing point depression: Karen Bennett, Quinn Clarke, Sally Cuckson, Frances Dickinson, Marie Dixon, Paul Dougherty, Margiad and Phillip Eckstein, Liz George, Cas Gorham, Lisa Graham, Joanne Hart, Jackie Heppard, Charlotte Hay, Catherine Heard, Connie Latshaw, Iwan LLewelyn Jones, Delyth Lloyd, Jackie Mcgrath, Carla Pinto, Lesley-Ann Reed and Lisa Taylor. My thanks also go to Albert Azzopardi of Fitter Clutch in Hoxton for managing to keep Mr. Frosty on the road, and to Tori Wynn and Sophia Gilliatt for their contribution to Mr.Frosty's maquillage. Finally, but not least, my thanks go to my mother and father for their enduring love and lifelong support.